PRIDE
IN THE
VOICES

HEATHER SPILLMAN

First published by On the Write Path Publishing
5023 W. 120th Ave. #228
Broomfield, CO 80020
martinmcleanlit@aol.com

On The Write Path
PUBLISHING

Paperback ISBN: 978-1-63837-046-8
eBook ISBN: 978-1-63837-047-5

This book is printed on acid-free paper.
Printed in the United States of America

Dedicated to all the people who let their rainbow light shine bright.

And to those on their journey to do so.

THANK YOUS

I would like to thank several people for helping me make this project happen:

First, I want to thank my husband for his amazing support of me and my (sometimes crazy) ideas and for being a great spellchecker and proofreader. I love you Jason, thank you.

Second, I'd like to thank my kids; my daughter who has been a terrific sounding board and supported this project from the start, and my son who cheered me on and was also a great spellchecker and proofreader. I love you both, thank you.

Third, I want to thank Michael Vrooman, my friend, my sounding board on this project and the all around amazing human he is, thank you.

BUT MOST OF ALL, I would like to thank every single person who is part of this book! Your willingness to put yourselves out there and share your experiences is incredibly brave and beautiful, thank you.

IN MEMORIAM

I would like to take a moment and remember the oldest contributor I have, Corky. We lost him to COVID-19 in the middle of writing this book. He was an icon in his own right and by his answers you can see he lived through some of the most significant times in LGBTQ+ history. I wanted to include a couple of correspondences I had with him which show why he chose to participate and supported this project.

"Hi Heather. Being 76, there are lots of questions I can add some input...some with only a sentence or two, others a bit longer, if you'd want that? I'll be working on it starting tomorrow, and get it back to you asap. Bless your heart for this undertaking trying to help our 'younger, up-and-coming' gay youths! One mother once said to me, 'Corky, these kids don't have a clue what you all had to go through!' With your help many will benefit from your book! Thanks for including me ♥ :-)!"

"Hi Heather. Just wanted to let you know...I haven't forgotten about you and your project! The question about the changes I have seen took lots of space since I've been around for so long. LOL ♥"

"FINALLY it's finished and sent to you! Again, I'm sorry it took so long and so rambling...it's also a book (or short story) in itself. Good luck and please keep me posted! With Love & Hugs ♥""

Corky, I hope you are dancing the freest you ever have! Thank you for sharing all of you always!

Let me introduce myself. My name is Heather, I am the mother of a member of the LGBTQ+ community and a fierce ally. As an ally, I show up to our state capitol when legislation is being brought, I help protect people at LGBTQ+ events with an incredible organization called Parasol Patrol, and I am a hugger! I give hugs at Pride events with Free Mom Hugs and an amazing thing happens when you provide a safe and loving hug, people tend to spill their personal truth and tell you their innermost secrets. The things I have whispered in my ear get me choked up but I refuse to let the tears fall in the moment, because I am there to be strong and loving to the person I'm hugging. When I get back into my car to go home, I sit for a moment and let the tears out and reflect on the hurt and loneliness and longing for acceptance that I heard that day.

I write this book using the real voices and life experiences from an amazing group of people willing to share their truth. This book will hopefully give lonely people a sense of belonging, and give family and friends, who do not accept a person as who they are, insight and understanding to maybe, just maybe change their minds. I also want to share good information for all of us to further our education in accepting people just as they are!

I have asked a good cross section of people from the LGBTQ+ community to answer a list of questions and I have kept them anonymous so they could be truthful without worry. Each is identified by a name, their age and how they identify (if they chose to reveal that). Every chapter title is one of the questions, and each chapter's content will go in order of age from oldest to youngest so you can see what the different eras have had to deal with, or if they are reaping the benefits of those who came before them. The age range is from 76 years old to 20 years old. Each person has their own life story, the place where they grew up, what their family is like, and what they have been through. Their personal stories are sure to have something that you will relate to in some way. I knew going in that I was asking people to feel something incredibly personal and step completely out of their comfort zone, but I was hopeful that the anonymity would give them free license to tell their story and it might even be cathartic for them. I did have a few people decline to participate, saying they couldn't "go back there again." I think this is an exclamation point on this project, and proof that the stories need to be told and shared to give something tangible to people, so they don't feel like they are the only one and that there is hope and good things to come. I did not require them to answer every question but kept them in the lineup, so to speak. In case you want to read just their story, you'll know where to find them in each chapter.

My intention for this book is to give those of you on your coming out journey, insights to see that you are not alone. My objective for this book is to give parents, friends and family of an LGBTQ+ person better enlightenment into the community. My purpose for this book is to give everyone a chance of understanding.

The people you will hear from are wonderfully diverse, incredibly giving of their voice and have three things in common. They are people who are productive members of society, they are a part of the LGBTQ+ community, and they have my love and respect and so much gratitude for their willingness to participate!

When I asked everyone to answer the questions, I told them to give me their favorite LGBTQ+ nonprofit so that a portion of the proceeds from this book could be donated. Here is a list of the nonprofits, some mentioned several times:

AIDS/Lifecycle

BTAC (Black Trans Advocacy Coalition)

Colorado AIDS Project

Colorado Gay Rodeo Association

Denver Gay Men's Chorus

Feeding Denver's Hungry

GDNAF (The Greg Dollgener Memorial AIDS fund)

Human Rights Campaign (2 times)

Imperial Court of the Rocky Mountain Empire

LGBT Center of LA

NGLTF

NOH8 Campaign

Parasol Patrol

Project Angel Heart (5 times)

Rocky Mountain CARES

SF AIDS Foundation

The Center on Colfax

The Matthew Shepard Foundation (4 times)

The Trevor Project (7 times)

Urban Peak

We Are Family Colorado Organization

One final note: I am an ally, but just saying that doesn't mean I'm done! I am learning and listening with my heart and mind open always. Promoting and working for equality is also part of being an ally. Respecting pronouns and using them correctly is being an ally. Correcting misinformation when you hear it or see it is being an ally. To be an ally we need to put the work in and I hope each of you join me. And being an ally is not just for straight people. A gay person helping a transgender person is being an ally, a lesbian speaking out on behalf of a non-binary person is being an ally, a drag queen being supported by her community is being an ally, etc.

Disclaimer—I am not an expert. I am just a mom who gives hugs and hears things.

Now sit back,
open your heart
and your mind,
and read.

Did you read the previous page?

CONTENTS

CHAPTER 1

WHEN AND HOW DID YOU KNOW?

CORKY
76
MR.

Like so many other gay & lesbians, I can think back to when I knew I was attracted to those of our own sex...about the age of 10 years old! My family went to see the movie, *Trapeze*, and I was so mesmerized by Tony Curtis...I remember thinking he was so handsome. When I was a senior in high school, I drove to Washington Park, where I had heard "gay guys" hung out...I found that to be correct and knew I was gay! Still very closeted, but after nights of going out with my straight friends, I'd get in my car and go cruising at Washington Park or around the Capitol Building, which was "the" place to connect with other gay guys.

DAVID
69
HE

I think that was about as soon as I knew about sexuality. My first friend and I started playing around in kindergarten. My friend saw it as "practicing" for sex with girls, but I knew that wasn't my case.

en I was in junior high school, just had been infatuated looking nude men.

ROB
66

I don't even really know. I knew I was different but I didn't even realize how.

CJEAN
63
HE/HIM

Being gay is NOT sex—That confusion by so many straight homophobes is why there is fear for children since they cannot distinguish between sexuality and orientation and think gay equates some danger to children. Many people are aware early on that they are "different." Society was quick to assign you gender roles and strict expectations that you fill them from birth—"What is it, a boy or a girl?" I preferred playing with the girls. I was actually good in sports like track and soccer until it became competitive, then I wanted nothing to do with the macho behavior. Sexually (this is MUCH later), I knew when I was attracted to muscle men in car magazines. The kicker was the model in a hair dryer owner's manual—hairy chest—woof—so funny now.

SHANNON
58

I first was attracted to another girl in 6th grade. I didn't fully accept that I was gay until my late 20s.

The Stonewall Uprising? The Marriage Equality Act? Something else?

TOM
58

I have been attracted to men for as long as I can remember.

TONY
58
HE/HIM

Well, looking back, I have always known. Even as a very young boy, I was always attracted to men. I remember first looking at "dirty" magazines with a neighbor boy (I was about 10), and I was most interested in the men and not the women. Of course I didn't tell my friend and had no idea what it all meant. In sixth grade, although I didn't know it at the time, I met my first "boyfriend." We will call him Jay. Jay and I held hands and were inseparable. It was more than 20 years later that we both talked about it and came out to each other officially. We remain friends today.

CHRISTOPHER
57

I always knew that I was "different." It took until puberty to begin to understand what that difference was. Even as far back as grade school, all of my friends were having crushes on girls. I was having crushes on boys.

GUS
57
HE/HIM

I think that at some level, I always knew. It wasn't until college that I acted upon my feelings. I was 17, and all these cute college guys were a real turn on, and I was finally away from my parents...over

p e Voices

niles away. I had my first same sex romance that year. After
, I was back under the influence of my parents and others that
pt me in the closet, and thought that there was NO WAY that I
ive the life of a gay man. There were so few, if any, role models
oked like me.

D

. I was in first grade, I was playing in the school yard with other
in my grade. We were playing "House" and I had to slide down
slide with a little girl, showing we were "married." When I did, I
ought to myself, "This doesn't feel right." Later in life, when in middle school, I had my first "encounter" with another boy and thought
to myself, "This feels right." That's how I knew I wasn't quite the
same as other boys.

ANTHONY
53
HE/HIM/HIS

I started to have feelings toward a man when I was 12 years old. I was
somehow attracted to this one particular man but he was married
with a baby.

JOHN
52
GAY MALE AND HE/HIM/HIS

I knew almost as soon as puberty started, and began experimenting
limitedly when I could in high school; however acknowledgement/
comfort would not come for many, many years (almost decades).

4

When and how did you know?

The Stonewall Uprising? The Marriage Equality Act? Something else?   200

MIKE
51
HE/HIM/HIS

I started being aware in sixth grade. All the girls in class thought a certain guy was cute, and so did I.

PASHA
51
SHE/HER OR THEY/THEM

When I was at least four, I watched *Gilligan's Island* and I had a huge crush on Ginger but she was the "nasty" one. I knew my feelings were "wrong," so I would make it overly clear that I thought Mary Ann was the best!

DAVID
50
HE/HIM

Looking back I think I always knew.

MICHAEL
50
HE/HIM/HIS

I think I knew I was gay at a pretty young age. My first intimate experience with the same sex was at age 13.

KIMMY
47
HIM/HER

I knew I was different by third grade but didn't know how at the time. I was a late bloomer but by my senior year of high school

I knew I was bisexual. I wasn't even thinking of gender issues back then but I was horribly sad. I felt that there was something wrong with me. That I was defective. I was in the mindset of guilt (Catholic), of fear (Catholic again and the new AIDS epidemic), and also, of constant stress in the hopes to fool everyone that I was straight.

JONATHAN
44
HE/HIM

I started having an inkling of knowing back in 1999. I was in college and I remember one night having this dream in which I made out with a guy. I also remember really enjoying that kiss. That dream set in motion my journey to figure out if this was a part of who I really was. This journey culminated in my officially coming out in the year 2000.

JV
43
HE/HIM/HIS

I was five or six when I knew I was attracted to men, not sexually yet, of course, but just infatuated.

KAYTI
LOOK 32, FEEL 78, LEGALLY 42
RECENTLY FEMALE (SHE/HER/HERS) TO EVERYONE BUT BLOOD FAMILY

Since I was three? I have tried to play dress up for over 35 years.

RYAN
39
HE/HIM

I knew from about the 6th grade, and it was more a feeling of knowing that something was different than anything else.

STEPHEN
38
HE/HIM

Started to suspect/fear through adolescence as I was attracted to other boys my age much like they were attracted to other girls our age. More certain of it, and even more fearful of it, through college.

ANDREW
30
PANSEXUAL TRANSGUY—HE/HIM

Started figuring out my sexuality in high school. In high school is when I started realizing that I was attracted to women as well as men. I went through a period of time in high school and the start of college unsure if I was bisexual or a lesbian (before accepting my gender identity). It wasn't until I was in college that the term pansexual and I found each other so to speak!

I started to question my gender identity about the same time puberty started; in short, it just didn't feel right, in the slightest! I was just not comfortable with not only what was going on, but with myself, completely! It wasn't until my senior year in high school, with the assistance/guidance of one of my teachers, I started to actually be able to articulate my struggles with my gender and be able to find the right path for me, my gender and ultimate transition. In college, the LGBTQ+ resource center on campus helped continue the journey of not only self-acceptance but ultimately for me, starting my transition to who I am today!

JACKSON
30
HE/HIM/HIS

I always knew I was different, never knew the proper term until a deep conversation with my wife one night in my late 20s.

MISS JESSICA
27
NON-BINARY, ALL PRONOUNS

I feel like I have always known, as I was surrounding myself with loving people and putting myself in spaces that were safe. I started believing in the things I was feeling and brought them full force.

PARRISH
23
HE/HIM

I knew going into my senior year of high school. I didn't want to believe it though; it was something I had buried deep down in my head and I think it came back to the surface as I was about to enter a new phase of my life. I didn't come out at this point though, but knew that I was going to spend my life with a guy.

MADI
21
SHE/HER

I knew in 5th grade. I don't know how, it's just something that I always knew about myself. It is hard for me to describe because it was just something that was part of me. I think I figured out exactly what it meant in 5th grade because I learned what the word "gay" actually meant. Before then, I just thought everyone was the same as me and assumed they all felt the same way.

FREYA
20
SHE/HER/HERS

I knew officially later in life during high school, but during my early years in elementary and middle school I always felt different. Everyone used to bully me for being weird in school and I felt weird. I think that is when I really knew.

***

If you ever wondered if being LGBTQ+ was a choice, I hope after reading this chapter you now realize that you were wrong. People know who they are, whether they can admit it, because of everything that it comes with at this point in history or not, it is not a choice.

CHAPTER 2

WHO DID YOU COME OUT TO? HOW DID IT GO? AT WHAT AGE? DESCRIBE HOW YOUR FAMILY REACTED WHEN YOU TOLD THEM.

CORKY
76
MR.

My oldest brother, who was 10 years older then me, was also gay and had come out to the entire family, including grandparents, when he was a teenager. Because of this I never actually "came out" to them, so I had "girlfriends" that never did more than making out. I didn't live at home after I graduated from high school and went to college in Durango/Greeley. During my senior year, at a gay party, I ran into a girl I had known in high school. She was also going to "Colorado State College" (now University of Northern Colorado) and we both graduated in 1967. We both began teaching in Denver Public Schools and moved into an apartment together. Late in that year, an angry girlfriend of hers threatened to call our parents and DPS, essentially "outing us," which meant we would lose our teaching jobs! The very next day we went to Denver Court House, obtained a license, and got married...all in the same day! I moved to San Francisco in June of 1970 and she moved there the next year. We'd live together, on and off, until '77 when we split and went our "own ways."

DAVID
69
HE

I was out to my college friends, starting late in my freshman year. No one was shocked.

I didn't tell them. My mother found a letter I had started to write to my best friend from college. I didn't finish it and I threw it in the trash...apparently in an orange juice can. Mother wanted to know what I was "trying to hide" so she pulled it out and read it. She told me to read the second chapter of Romans. I told her I had and suggested she reread the first. She later insisted that I see a psychologist. I told her I had and suggested that she might want to see one. She was not amused. One of my brothers suggested that I see his wife's psychologist who also happened to be a Methodist minister. He told me to "discuss baseball scores or whatever" just to placate my mother. I went to see him, and we mostly talked about my mother. We both agreed she wouldn't see him so there was no point in even discussing it. When I got home, Mother asked about my appointment. I said it was okay and that the psychologist was a nice guy. Then she asked when I was going to see him again. I said I wasn't. She asked if that was my decision or his. I told her we both agreed that I really hadn't needed to see him in the first place. A week or so later, I was going to see a friend in a nearby town. Mom came out to the car and told me that I was doing it because I "didn't love" her. I said, "Lady, that's bullshit and you know it." (the only time I ever swore at my mother.)

When I got back she'd calmed down. I think she talked to some of my siblings and they basically said, "Didn't you know that already? We did." Mother took a little more educating over the years, but she caught on pretty fast. The only thing my father said to me (I know it was because Mother said he had to talk to me about it) was, "Son, I think you're old enough to have outgrown this by now." The subject never came up again. After that though, every time I was home, Dad and I (frequently with organization help from my mother) would spend at least one afternoon riding around the farm and general neighborhood in his pickup truck. We always had a great time.

JW
66

My mother confronted me about a letter my big sister had read from a married man when I was about 14 or 15 so I guess I came out to her only, not my father. My mother wasn't upset. She just said that you know your father is a pretty straight arrow headed man and you know your dad would be really upset with you, so it's best not to tell him.

My mother seemed fine with it, but I did not come out to my dad until my mother had passed away and he said he knew already. I guess maybe he sensed it, but he said you're my one and only son and I don't love you any less. He was a little disappointed but he still loved me.

ROB
66

I don't remember coming out to anybody. I just started living my life. I didn't need a speech to do that.

My parents were already dead by the time I'd come out to myself.

CJEAN
63
HE/HIM

It's a process, not a singular event. I tend to think about being 18 when I met some gay friends and they took me to my first gay bar. A very early bear bar Cuddles on drag night—one performer had just finished gender reassignment surgery (sex change at the time) and was wearing crotch-less panties. I was not even phased and knew I would fit in somehow as gay. It was the least traumatic experience to feel at home—it all fell into place and made sense. I came out to friends first, then family and finally at my job.

In my teens, I spoke with my mother about my unusual feelings and she had me speak to the doctor she worked for. He said it was a phase, even football quarterbacks went through. I tried to ignore it. Oddly, my biggest regret was not taking the quarterback up on it when he made passes at me in high school.

When I finally came out to my mother, I was trying to have a conversation with her without actually saying it and she finally asked, "You're not one of those, are you?" I said, "Yes" and I can still see the scene, somehow in black and white—the back of her hand to her forehead as she fainted and slid down the wall, crumbled on the floor. It was hours of crying and blame and guilt and talking. It took years for her to come around and eventually she referred to my husband (not legally back then) at the time as another son. One sister said no big deal, the other wasn't as forthcoming. My father would ask when I was going to "straighten up" and I told him to go do some research and leave me alone. My niece and nephew called my ex Uncle Gary.

SHANNON
58

I didn't come out to anyone that wasn't gay until I was 40. I told my siblings around then and told my parents several years later.

My siblings were supportive. My parents were a different story. I wrote my parents a letter to tell them. My mom wrote back and told me that she wasn't surprised and that she loved me and knew it wasn't something that I had chosen. My dad wrote me and told me that we would agree to disagree and that we would not discuss it and that he loved me. They have been very loving toward Jenny and the kids and treat them as if they are their grandchildren and daughter-in-law.

TOM
58

I came out to my parents when I was 40. Astonishingly, they had no idea that I was gay. They were very supportive, but I was a mess. I felt like I was disappointing them. I still feel that way to this day. I am the last male in our family. Our family name ends with me. I feel like a failure.

They were very supportive. My sister and especially my brother-in-law were incredibly supportive.

TONY
58
HE/HIM

I had to come out a few times, first to myself, then my friends, then my family. Throughout high school and college, my attraction to men grew stronger and more cognizable, but I did everything to suppress my feelings. I was very involved in the church during high school and convinced myself that the Bible said no premarital sex with women, but God didn't say anything about men. So, men were fair game. I experimented with a few friends in high school. It was exhilarating and terrifying. I felt enormous guilt after each experience. In college, I had two very serious boyfriends. Again, I didn't admit it at the time, but they were very real. When things got too serious, I responded "but I am not gay" (never mind that we have been sleeping together and having great sex). But when it came to "falling in love" I went running. I hurt them both very very deeply. Years after my official coming out (which I am getting to) I tracked each of them down and apologized for being such a shit. "Karl" listened but was not very forgiving. "Jeff" was forgiving and we were able to be friends. I have lost touch with them now, but will never forget them. Indeed, I had fallen in love and I often wonder how life might have unfolded had I been out and true to myself at that time.

Post college, at 24, I was living near Denver in a townhome my dad helped me buy. I had experimented with men, but it was always fleeting and never serious. But the feelings were growing more and more. I was dating a woman at the time, and she had a good friend who was gay. The three of us went to a gay bar and wow! I whispered to him, "I feel at home here." But I kept it from my girlfriend. A few months later, I was hosting a party, got drunk, and was making out with a guy when my girlfriend walked in. Yikes. Yes, I needed to confront me, but my religious upbringing said it was wrong. At that time in 1986, AIDS was in the daily news and news accounts were of men having "hundreds of sexual partners" which didn't describe me at all, so I couldn't be gay if that is what it meant to be gay, right? I wanted a relationship. I had no role models.

There was a fateful and very tear-filled day in 1986. I was sitting on my bed, took the gun out of my desk, and held it on my chest. I really did want to end the pain and I just sobbed. I can't actually recall all that went through my mind in those moments. I knew I was in remarkable pain and wanted it to end, but something else must have been telling me it would be okay. I held the gun up, looked at it closely, and said...not today. I put the gun away, walked to the bathroom mirror, looked at myself and said, "You are gay, get over it." I had to say the words out loud, "I am gay."

My friends would later tell me that I not only knocked down the closet doors, but also busted down the front doors too. I came out strongly in that moment, and have lived out and proud since.

Coming out to myself was the first big step. As I started to confide in friends, more than a few said, well I knew, I am glad you now do. I wish someone would have told me, but I would have likely denied it. In any event, I had more support than I realized. I wasn't interested in having people in my life that were not okay with my being gay. Indeed, it was a defining time. I moved closer to the "gay" part of town (Capitol Hill area of Denver) and began to make new friends.

I still "hid" who I was at work and from family for some time. It would be more than a year before I would get the courage to come out to my mom. She and my dad were visiting and I took my mom out for a drink. I talked around the issue for some time saying, "Mom, do you have any idea where I am going with this?" Of course she said "no." Then minutes later the lightbulb lit up and she asked, "Are you gay?" I had to say the words again, "Yes, Mom, I am gay." We cried and she told me how proud she was and said how difficult that had to be for me. We agreed she would tell my dad. She did after the trip, leading up to it by saying, "Wasn't it a good trip? Wasn't Tony happy? Well, there is a reason for that." My dad, however, wasn't as understanding. It would be about a year before he would talk to me. And that's another story.

So, early on, my mom was quite the ally. Dad, a different story. He would tell me, "Being gay and with the whole AIDS thing is like a moth to a flame, eventually you are going to get burned." Well, thanks for the support, Dad. But, I had to give him room. It took me nearly 24 years to come out to myself, I could give him some time to understand. I was adopted so I told him, "Look it's genetic, you had nothing to do with it." I don't think he appreciated the attempt at humor. Eventually, he would come around. My first very serious relationship was with someone whose family "disowned" him when they learned he was gay and in a relationship with me. My dad was heartbroken by that and told me, "That's okay, he is now our second adopted son."

For years, my sister believed I was doing it "for the attention." Yep, that's it. I want attention so I am going to pretend to be gay, experience all sorts of discrimination and hostility, all to get the attention of my parents? Ugh. But, years later she would come around, too.

Things would get complicated. Although my parents and sister attended the ceremony with my first serious partner (marriage wasn't legal then) and my parents would attend my marriage to my current husband, they also voted against gay marriage in California. Needless to say, the relationship has been complicated. Their religion really got in the way.

CHRISTOPHER
57

I struggled with my sexuality until my early 20s. I went into the U.S. Navy at 17, which in the early 1980s was extremely challenging, as it was years before "don't ask, don't tell" would come about. I suppressed that aspect of myself for most of the first four years I served. During my second four year tour, I came to terms with myself and mastered living a dual existence, half of me in two different worlds. I came out to my parents a couple of years after leaving the military, I was 27, after dreading what my father's reaction would be. I was the oldest son of the oldest son for four generations of an Irish catholic family. I didn't know how to tell my father that it ended with me. As it turned out, I underestimated my father. He was a little shaken and said he would need some time to digest what I had told him, but he made it clear that while he did not yet understand fully, he didn't love me any less. My mother was a nurse, and as I learned then, always knew. She told me that she was just waiting for ME to figure it out.

GUS
57
HE/HIM

I was 38, married to a woman for 12 years, and with two young children (8 and 2 yrs old). I came out, through therapy, to a counselor that I had been sent to by the minister of the church we were attending, following very unsuccessful marriage counseling. Coming out wasn't the hard part. Facing the rest of my "life" (wife, kids, family and friends) and admitting that I hadn't been my genuine self, was the most difficult thing I've ever done, or will ever do.

Disdain (how could you do this?). Disbelief (how could you have fathered two children?) Distancing (my siblings and I have never talked about my coming out, even after all these years. Today, I don't really talk to any of them).

BRAD
54

I didn't technically "come out." I was "found out" by the administration at the Christian college I was attending. They, in turn, called my parents and told them their findings, of my "promiscuity." It was quite terrifying. *How did it go?* Not well. I was dismissed from college six weeks before graduation. *At what age?* 22 years old.

My family was not very accepting of me. I was starting a relationship and brought my first husband, Chris, to a family gathering. They didn't know how to react. Eventually, my sister told my mother that she needed to either accept me and Chris or alienate me from the family by not accepting us. They eventually started warming up to him after 10 years together. He started to really become part of the family before his passing, after 24 years together.

ANTHONY
53
HE/HIM/HIS

I came out to my best friend in the 9th grade when I was 14 years old.

I told my sister first who had already figured it out who then told my mom. My mom was very upset about the situation. We waited several more years before telling my dad who was not upset about it at all.

JOHN
52
GAY MALE AND HE/HIM/HIS

The first person I ever came out to was a friend. *How did it go?* Fine, they were very understanding/supportive/not set back.

At what age? Late 20s.

Understanding and as supportive as they could be given that it was pretty far out of their sociodemographic norm at the time.

19

MIKE
51
HE/HIM/HIS

I came out to a friend who told me another guy at a party was interested in me, then other friends and then my family.

When I told my mom she cried. She was afraid life would be harder for me and was upset that probably I wouldn't be having children for her to be a grandmother to.

PASHA
51
SHE/HER OR THEY/THEM

I was 15 when I came out to friends and had my first girlfriend.

I'm only out to my sister. I'm estranged from my entire family except my mother, with whom I occasionally text. My sister took it well at the time. We've since had a falling out about an unrelated issue.

DAVID
50
HE/HIM

I think it was an old friend. It went well, she is gay as well. I was 25. I met a guy at Tracks and ended up going home with him.

Well my mom was upset and cried and my dad said, "Well…I kind of figured." Lol. My sisters both were cool about it. Told me that it was okay. And I don't even know if my brother knows that I am gay.

MICHAEL
50
HE/HIM/HIS

My mother *How did it go?* It was hard but a mother usually knows before you tell them. She was understanding, although probably worried at first how difficult my life would be after announcing my decision. She said she would always love me and forever has.

At what age? 18

My Parents had been divorced since I was 3 years old. My biological father did not accept it or understand. A devout, church going man, my father said that it was not allowed, had me come out and spend time with him and went as far as telling me I was going to Hell for "making this decision." Before he passed, we met on common ground and all was good between us.

KIMMY
47
HIM/HER

I am Gender Queer/Gender nonconforming or nonbinary. I like the term two spirited but since I am not indigenous I would feel cagey to use that. I came out at 45. I showed a pic of me in drag to my best friend and he laughed at me and walked away. A few days later things were back to normal and he was talking to me again. Since I have only a couple friends in real life (not including the virtual friends on FB) I am still friends with him even though he thinks I am a joke.

I never directly came out to my family. When I was around 12, my dad once said in conversation that he didn't care what I did as long as I wasn't a fag or a Muslim. I remembered that comment and at 15, after getting frisky for the first time with another boy, I felt I had to stay in the closet. I only had two other experiences with guys during my late teens. I married my girlfriend at age 22, and was married for about 15 years but we were separated by my mid 30s. We were a typical artsy, punk rocker/goth couple with typical bills to pay. We both agreed that we had failed expectations of each other and after nearly 15 years, we needed to end it. When I met my wife (through friends while clubbing) life was getting to be good and I was close to opening up about swinging both ways to my friends and also how crossdressing gave me some crazy feelings. But, when you meet that person who you really, really like and you fall in love you think that's it. My orientation is a choice. I choose to be with this person. I like them, they have a cute ass and we have the same kinds of ideas about things. We fall in love and plan to flee from Central New York, flee our circle of friends who don't appear to be going anywhere. We stopped clubbing and moved in with each other and had a basic hetero-rela-tionship. After our marriage ended, I casually dated women and had a couple FWBs but was always hoping to find a boyfriend, even if it was just a casual thing but it never happened. It was my own fault because I was still maintaining a straight persona due to fear. That fear of being outed. Fear that I may actually get what I want and with that; all my illusions and barriers would be knocked down and the real me would be exposed to the world and there is no going back.

I had crossdressed a little in my late teens/early 20s (1991-94). I hung out with a couple cool chicks who were happy to draw eyeliner on me. They would give me black fishnets to accommodate my dad's old combat boots and my cutoff jeans that were held together with safety pins and anarchy paraphernalia. Clubbing in the early 90s was the best time of my life up to then. I got exposed to many different kinds of people and music. I learned to spot and avoid the uncool people who lurked in the dark corners of the clubs.

At the age of 45, I started to crossdress again and play with cosmetics. I started posting pics of me crossdressing at several dance parties and just let the questions roll throughout my social media and my mother. That is how I came out so to speak. I never came out directly. I posted pics. My only explanation was ... I like to dance in drag and I like whomever I like. I'm a philosophy geek who never gives anyone direct answers. I answer questions by saying...consider this if you will. When my mother called asking if "this is a thing?" referring to a FB post of me dressed as Magenta from Rocky Horror Picture Show. She asked if it was a thing. I said, to which thing are you referring? I have 20 "things." I wanted to make her ask it directly. To answer her question I stated that I am neither a boy or girl in my mind. Some days I express myself one way, other days I express myself differently. Since I was a punk rocker in my teens, she was used to me wearing eyeliner and nail polish to go clubbing. I also had girlfriends so most of the time I looked like a typical white trash punk rocker male but had a steady job after school and a club life that I was so busy that the conversation never came up. I was hardly home once I bought a car at 16.

Now, because of the stigma with bisexuality which hung around me like an albatross, I moved out after graduating high school, got married as I stated above, and distanced myself as much as I could from my whole family. I tried to deny my truth to everyone and myself. I was happy being married but I hated myself a little.

My dad died in the summer of 97. My mom, being a source of a lot of my childhood stress as well as my adult depression, still lives in Central New York and we talk more these days but we still have our unresolved issues.

I use my FB as a tool to force the conversation. Not just with my mother but to everyone I know—on my terms. I also use my social media to let them know.

This is me.

There are others like me.

I no longer give a fuck what others think because life is too short to be anything less than what I am.

Despite having my ups and downs, I am, relatively speaking, the happiest I have ever been.

JONATHAN
44
HE/HIM

The very first person I remember coming out to was my good friend Kristen. One night I got into my car and just drove. I drove around town for a good couple of hours just thinking and trying to put all my feelings into some kind of coherent order. Finally arriving at Kristen's house, I told her I had something important to share with her. Well, three tequila shots later, I came out to my very first person. It went very well and she was extremely supportive.

Being from a Hispanic family there was always the fear that I wouldn't be accepted. When I told my family, it was more of a "finally you told us despite us knowing already" reaction than a negative one. I remember specifically telling my mom and her reply was very succinct, "I know, now let's go have dinner." I was 24.

JV
43
HE/HIM/HIS

College Best Friend. He was already out and I had a secret crush on him. I then came out as BI. *How did it go?* It went really well, we were able to confide in each other and soon so many others followed suit. We were at a very Bible Belt Southern Baptist university at that.

At what age? 21.

My dad had just passed a few months before I came out. I come from a very religious background. Dad was a Southern Baptist preacher my early life from grade school to college. I came out to my two older brothers first, they pretty much knew and were very supportive. My sister was super young and was mostly scared for me, not knowing what it truly meant. Now we're best friends, and my 17-year-old neice, her daughter, pretty much identifies as gay. As a few other of my family members as well. Mom back then didn't truly believe it was from God. But only knowing faith and prayer my whole life I had given my heart to God and pleaded if it wasn't his will to take it away. My mom's side of the family is Assembly of God and I always believed I was going to hell. I finally asked my mom, "Did you and dad ever know?" She said they've known since I was 5, that I was different. She's come around. Loves my husband and treats him like family. She still doesn't condone our marriage but says she loves us no matter what. Which she told me the night I came out to her. I said that's all I need.

KAYTI
LOOK 32, FEEL 78, LEGALLY 42
RECENTLY FEMALE (SHE/HER/HERS) TO EVERYONE BUT BLOOD FAMILY

Originally—My childhood sweetheart.

How did it go?—We are still friends.

At what age? Under age 5.

They don't appreciate it. They have shamed me many times over the years. My mother refuses to acknowledge, "If you had been born a girl, your name would be _____."

RYAN
39
HE/HIM

I did not come out to my immediate family until I was 25, and it was not a great experience. I had been living very openly in my personal life, but I did not speak my truth to my family. So, when it came to fruition, there were many hard feelings for my lack of openness and honesty with them.

My family was hurt that I had not been open and honest with them, but they have always been supportive.

STEPHEN
38
HE/HIM

I told a friend somewhere around junior year of college at age 21. She had been my friend since we were three years old and my prom date senior year of high school. But the language I used at the time (and would for a long time) was that I was "struggling with my sexuality and didn't want to be gay." She was loving and accepting of my struggle, though clearly I wasn't asking her to accept more beyond that, because I wasn't accepting more beyond that.

I also told my parents the same "struggle" not long after that, the summer before senior year of college. My mom cried, but hugged me and said she loved me no matter what and would always be praying for me. At the time, she was praying for me to find a woman and fall in love. Dad got angry and told me I should then really consider changing my major (I was getting my degree in Middle School Math and Science Education) because I shouldn't be around children. I was stunned as he's way more level-headed than this. Thankfully, it took him 24 hours to come around and apologize and tell me he overreacted and loved me no matter what. He surprisingly didn't put any caveat on that. But we also didn't talk about my sexuality again for over a decade.

ANDREW
30
PANSEXUAL TRANSGUY—HE/HIM

In high school, my sexuality (at the time) was out there. Family and friends pretty much all knew at about the same time. All of them also were pretty accepting.

My gender identity was slower to start. It was only the one teacher and maybe one or two other people while I was in high school who had any idea this was something I was struggling with. While I was a freshmen in college, I was honored enough to be in a LGBTQ peer group through the resource center; they all knew and were all supportive moving forward! Once I came out to my college theatre department, sophomore year, they were all pretty accepting. Took a bit for everyone to get the name and pronouns down but they all did get there! Luckily I've not had many issues within the theatre community or work, even after college. But I am also guarded on who I tell, since even I have had a few instances that it was an issue (even as minor as it may have been).

My pansexuality though is on the down low however. I have never felt the super need to tell everyone about it. Some people just either think I am straight or gay depending on the situation; and I only tell people again depending on the situation. I just don't have an overwhelming urge to tell either one to anyone/everyone but I am also not ashamed to share either when called for.

My family was a bit harder! My mom was the one who I told first. She was taken aback, surprised to say the least. She was not mad or anything to that extent but was not expecting this at all. Took her time to fully accept and adjust to but she ultimately did! What took me by surprise actually was her familiarity with being transgender; all thanks to the fairly recent (at the time of me coming out to her as trans) coverage of Chaz Bono (she grew up watching Sonny and Cher, so it ultimately made sense, I was just not prepared for it in the moment). This happened between my sophomore and junior year of college. I told my sister and brother-in-law pretty quickly after telling my mom. That was over the phone since they live in a different state. That conversation was pretty seamless—they had questions but were ultimately understanding.

My dad was a bit harder, only because the concept of transgender was a new one for him so he had more questions that he asked to help him understand. I was more nervous to tell him because he also comes from a catholic background. I'll admit that my mom had urged me to tell him since he was in a way, the last person for me to tell and I was putting it off; there was almost a year gap between telling my mom and my dad. But I did finally call him and told him eventually and he (and my whole family) did come around and support me! Which is unique because not all who are trans have this, especially when part (if not whole) of their family is catholic.

JACKSON
30
HE/HIM/HIS

I first came out to close family in April of 2018, then I took to sharing it publicly with friends and social media. It went well at first, until the world recognized my truth...then it became increasingly harder.

Most of my family took me coming out as transgender well, not shocked. Of course, there were a few difficult conversations to have.

I lost a few along the way, but I also gained some very close relationships who are like family now.

MISS JESSICA
27
NON-BINARY, ALL PRONOUNS

I came out to my family when I was 23 and the drag world when I was
23. It didn't go well with my family (excluding my sisters). It went
amazing with everyone else outside of my family.

My dad still hasn't spoken to me and/or looks at me, my mom was
trying for awhile and then stopped, and then my sisters and extended
family were super accepting.

PARRISH
23
HE/HIM

I came out to my best friend first, it was really terrifying. I didn't even
state that I was gay the first time. I said that I was seeing a couple
girls (I wasn't, I just thought it would help ease the blow I felt like I
was giving) and then I mentioned that I was seeing a guy too. That
same week, I told her again that I was really happy seeing this guy
and that I was gay. I am fortunate to have such a wonderful best
friend that is supportive and loving no matter what. I was 18 when I
came out.

I went into telling my family knowing that no matter what I said,
at the very least, I would be happy. It didn't matter to me if they
would accept me or not. With that being said, I do have very supportive parents that do accept and love me. I actually told my dad first at
dinner after he came up to see me in the show at college. I mentioned
that I was seeing a guy and that we didn't need to talk about it right

then. I think a week later, I was home for a weekend about to go back to school and I asked him to talk right before I left. He was very open, listened, and allowed me to be me. I think that was the most important thing, he listened and heard his son happy for who he is.

MADI
21
SHE/HER

The first person I came out to was my friend in 8th grade. I was really going through it in my head, and needed someone to know so that I didn't feel so alone. I told her and she was so supportive of me which made me feel really loved and happy. She convinced me to tell my family, and I did so in a Chick-fil-A of all places, LOL.

My family at first was a bit confused by what I said. They weren't sure that I really knew yet, and were curious about "how I knew" without having any experiences. It was hard for me to describe the fact that it was just something I knew, and that it wasn't something that I just discovered or wanted to be. It would be like if I asked someone how they knew they were straight. You just know.

FREYA
20
SHE/HER/HERS

I came out to Mom. It was so calm and safe. I was scared and cried but she was so supportive and loving. She gave me so much love and reassured me. I was 16 years old.

My family was so loving and happy for me. My mom told me she always knew and was just happy I finally came out of my shell. My sisters were loving and so excited for me. They all wanted to meet my girlfriend immediately.

Who did you come out to? How did it go? At what age? Describe how your family reacted when you told them.

***

I hope these very personal stories resonate and show that coming out is a process and that being surrounded by loving and caring family and community is the best thing. Find your loving and caring community, they are there; you just have to look! Be a loving, caring person accepting of all. It's not hard at all.

CHAPTER 3

DID YOU TRY ANY HETEROSEXUAL RELATIONSHIPS? HOW FAR DID YOU GO? DATING? MARRIAGE? DESCRIBE THE SITUATION.

CORKY
76
MR.

DAVID
69
HE

I did go out with a few girls in high school and college and even got into bed with a couple of them. Neither experience went well for either of us. I quickly decided to stop pretending.

JW
66

I was never in a heterosexual relationship as I felt or lets say the image I had of what a girl might want was a big butch man with lots of muscles and I was just a tall skinny dude. I did not have a very good self image of myself. I did have lots of girlfriends as in just friends, nothing real serious.

ROB
66

Yes, but not going there...this is painful.

CJEAN
63
HE/HIM

Never more than kissing a girl once—I am a "gold gay"—far 6 on Kinsey scale—never even tempted—I was clueless what to do since there was no attraction.

SHANNON
58

I nearly married a man two different times. Once, in college and then another man when I was in my late 20s.

TOM
58

I dated a couple of women in high school and college for appearance's sake (prom). It didn't go well as I wasn't into it. I've never had sex with a woman. I never got too involved, because I knew I didn't want to ruin someone else's life down the road. They didn't understand my low involvement and they didn't know I was gay. There were lots of misunderstandings. However, I am still very good friends to this day with one woman from that time.

TONY
58
HE/HIM

Yes, dating, no sex. I am a proud virgin with women. While I had a couple of girlfriends in high school, when it got serious, time to end it. College girlfriend described above. We remain friends today.

CHRISTOPHER
57

During my eight years in the military, I was paranoid about how I was perceived, so I did date several women during that time, to maintain appearances. One or two of them did involve some physical intimacy, but it was very sporadic. I felt guilty dating them as I felt I was using them. I did care about them, but not in the way that they were looking for. None of them lasted long for that reason.

GUS
57
HE/HIM

BRAD
54

Yes. *How far did you go?* Almost engaged to one girl. *Dating?* Yes. *Marriage?* No. *Describe the situation.* Very awkward. Uncomfortable. We weren't very physical at all, more like friends.

ANTHONY
53
HE/HIM/HIS

I kissed a girl once in the 6th grade. Once I knew I was gay, I had a pretend girlfriend which helped me in high school not get too bullied.

JOHN
52
GAY MALE AND HE/HIM/HIS

Yes.

How far did you go? I have had sex with women if that is the question.

Dating? Yes, though very few lengthy or substantial relationships.

MIKE
51
HE/HIM/HIS

I was lucky to come out at 16, so I only had dated a little and hadn't had sex yet.

PASHA
51
SHE/HER OR THEY/THEM

I don't really like to set a label on myself except perhaps, "Queer." I was out to my husband and everyone with no problems other than the typical passive aggressive judgment expected from even liberals nowadays.

DAVID
50
HE/HIM

I did try them and dating. It always turned out to be awkward and never went anywhere. I do have very limited physical experience sexually.

MICHAEL
50
HE/HIM/HIS

Yes. How far did you go? Almost engaged. *Dating?* Nothing serious prior to the almost engagement. *Marriage?* No. *Describe the situation.* I was with my last girlfriend until I was 21. Although I had come out to my family, I still dated and in her, found a true friend. I truly loved her but could not move forward in a lie. I went as far as telling her that I was gay and that seemed to be fine with her. Our friendship was very strong. Having been a product of divorce in my life, I knew that I could never put a child through what I had been through if I could avoid it. I ended the relationship and never dated a woman again.

KIMMY
47
HIM/HER

JONATHAN
44
HE/HIM

Yes. I did have heterosexual relationships. Looking back, let's just say they were awkward at best. I will leave it at that, lol!

JV
43
HE/HIM/HIS

I was in two serious hetero relationships but never sexual. *How far did you go?* Kissing. *Dating? Marriage? Describe the situation.* It was very interesting. I never felt anything sexual, even when we kissed. One was 9th grade and the second was in my junior/senior year.

KAYTI
LOOK 32, FEEL 78, LEGALLY 42
RECENTLY FEMALE (SHE/HER/HERS) TO EVERYONE BUT BLOOD FAMILY

Yes. *How far did you go? Dating? Marriage? Describe the situation.* I was married to a CIS female for 3.5 years, together for 12.5. They passed away. She tolerated my dressing but I don't feel that she encouraged it in a supportive way.

RYAN
39
HE/HIM

I had dated females through high school and college. However, I am very fortunate that it did not go any further than that.

STEPHEN
38
HE/HIM

I tried dating girls through college, I think two—three girls, and a handful of dates. I didn't really date in grad school. I then moved from Arkansas to Denver, CO and ended up dating one more time and married her a year later. We were married for three years and divorced.

ANDREW
30
PANSEXUAL TRANSGUY—HE/HIM

I have had a few heterosexual relationships over the years. Have not gotten to marriage yet, but perhaps someday? With that, I've minimized dating for a while because I wanted to get myself in a solid spot before I bring someone else into the mix because as a transguy, I understand that I come with some baggage.

JACKSON
30
HE/HIM/HIS

I did have a couple significant relationships with males when I was younger, however; they both have since come out as homosexual males.

MISS JESSICA
27
NON-BINARY, ALL PRONOUNS

Yeah! I've dated many girls and I still would! Being queer, I love humanity and am attracted to humanity. I just ultimately saw myself living happily with a man.

PARRISH
23
HE/HIM

I did try heterosexual relationships and a more serious one in high school. That went on for about eight months. She was amazing and we actually talk sometimes now, but when we were dating, there was something that just didn't feel "right." I knew this was something that wouldn't last deep down without sacrificing who I am and I would always be unhappy. When I was with her, it never crossed my mind that I was gay. Like I've said before, being gay was something I buried so deep down in my head.

MADI
21
SHE/HER

If you count my "boyfriend" I had in 7th grade, then yes, but the only time we ever "went on a date" was when I went to his birthday party with his friends. Long story short, I have not been in a heterosexual relationship. LOL.

FREYA
20
SHE/HER/HERS

I never did. I was always close to boys when I was younger and played with them the most during my early school years. I however never had a relationship with a boy.

***

As this is a very intimate question, I wasn't sure if I would get answers for it. Most who tried some sort of hetero relationship did so to keep up appearances. When will people just be able to pursue and love who they want? Love is love.

39

HAVE YOU EVER HAD TO HIDE YOUR TRUE SELF FROM YOUR FAMILY? FROM YOUR EMPLOYER? FROM SOMEONE ELSE?

CORKY
76
MR.

DAVID
69
HE

When I started working, I did feel that I had to hide the fact I was gay. I worked in what has been characterized as the world's most homophobic profession. I learned not to bring up sexual matters of any kind with coworkers and other strangers. In later jobs, most of my coworkers knew that I was gay but it seldom if ever came up. Very seldom did conversations involve an allusion to my sexuality, and never more than a brief one.

JW
66

I only had to hide my true self with my big sister, the one that found the letter when I was young and read it and told my mother (always stuck her nose in other people's business where it did not belong). She ended up getting married, changed religions and became a strict Southern Baptist girl and she did not like me for what I was. She always tried to preach to me and had two little girls at the time and did not want them to know anything bad that I was. So I had to act like a straight dude (brother).

ROB
66

Somewhat, but basically by omission.

CJEAN
63
HE/HIM

In my time, of course. I never lied but didn't tell either. I eventually came out to family, on the job, and most everyone that mattered to me. I have taken a job with a Catholic organization and feel compelled to keep my personal life to myself—it limits me in ways not being totally open. It's not a secret, but not open either. It saddens me that it's a step backwards.

SHANNON
58

I was a monster of music in Southern Baptist churches for 17 years. I was closeted to my employers and family. It was a very difficult time. I used to have major anxiety over it all. I was in relationships with women, but we stayed hidden. I finally got a teaching degree so I could leave church employment. I stayed in the closet my first few years of teaching. Once Jenny and I got married, I came out to everyone in my life at work and my family.

TOM
58

Yes, I hid my true self from my family and my employer until the last few years. Basically I hid it from everyone, most importantly I hid it from myself, or at least I tried to. I led two lives for 40 years: a straight life and a separate gay life. It was exhausting, mentally and emotionally. I aged tremendously leading this double life.

TONY
58
HE/HIM

Oh hell yes. It was the only way I thought to survive. The energy wasted being in the closet was exhausting. Talking about my "girl" friend who was a boy. Changing his name to Rene at work. Avoiding any topic at all cost to avoid disclosing details which could lead someone to know. I could only bring so much of myself to work or to family or some acquaintances. Truly authentic relationships were not really possible. Back in the day, the advice from my "mentors" was don't come out, it could be the end of your job. Indeed, I did lose a job because I was gay (of course not the stated reason).

But when I got political, I would never retreat to the closet again. Never. And, boy, did I find it powerful to be out in the workplace. Early on, so many would say, I didn't know I knew anyone gay. That created space for conversation and changes in people's perceptions. It is easy to discriminate or react negatively when you don't know something. Being out at work and in graduate (law) school was some of the most powerful activism in which I have engaged.

CHRISTOPHER
57

Yes and yes. See above for the family part. The only job that I had to masquerade for was the military. During the 1980s, being homosexual was not only culturally unacceptable, it was a court martialable offense and could end with a dishonorable discharge. During deployed periods at sea, it could be extremely dangerous to be "found out." The military was incessant about "rooting out" homosexuals and there were always "witch hunts" going on to entrap people, so invisibility was crucial.

GUS
57
HE/HIM

Up until 2000, yes. Even in college, I kept my several relationships a secret. It was the early 80s, and even the LGBT group on campus met in secret. After coming out, which was greatly facilitated by being "outed" to our friends and neighbors, I slowly came out to the professional friends that I trusted. It wasn't until nearly 10 years later that I felt comfortable being "out" at work.

BRAD
54

Yes, in the beginning of my "coming out" phase. *From your employer?* Yes, in Texas and Oklahoma.

ANTHONY
53
HE/HIM/HIS

Once my parents knew, I never hid my true identity. I was always open with my employer and co-workers.

JOHN
52
GAY MALE AND HE/HIM/HIS

I certainly spent years hiding my true self from literally everyone, including me. I want to add here that while I understand where the question is derived from, I do not think it is fair necessarily to phrase with the word had to. I think that all gay people spend some time in a closet of sorts, some barely at all and some for huge portions of their lives. Until the day or time arrives that you are ready to come out, you choose for a variety of reasons to hide who you are.

I am carrying on in this manner because in hindsight, I learned that I did not have to hide myself but that for too many emotional, physical, social reasons etc. I chose to. In the end, even for gay people who suffer terribly by loss of jobs, the support of housing or family and friends. And sadly, much of this does happen but in spite of all this really, we choose to hide, we do not have to. We often, for valid reasons think we have/had to but at the end of the line, it is a choice we make and made. Whether for good reason or not.

I offer this only as part of my perspective and not as a criticism or argumentative point of view but merely as a point of view which I believe is your objective here. Hopefully this is helpful in this overarching research goal.

MIKE
51
HE/HIM/HIS

Not hide, but not volunteer that I was gay.

44

Have you ever had to hide your true self from your family?
From your employer? From someone else?

PASHA
51
SHE/HER OR THEY/THEM

I definitely hid everything from my family when I was a child and teenager. However, as an adult, I haven't felt the need to have a big reveal. I know how they'll react and I'm 100% positive they know but they want to live in denial. If I had more contact with them, I'd definitely bring it up, for now I don't share any of my life with them much less my love life. I've worked as a DV Counselor for seven years, a sex worker, a church secretary at a UCC church and have been out in all of them.

DAVID
50
HE/HIM

Not from my family so much. In the workforce I was always pretty wary about it. Some employers were just fine with it. But you know there's always a coworker that has an issue.

MICHAEL
50
HE/HIM/HIS

No. *From your employer?* Yes, as a teenager in the 80s, it was not acceptable to be openly gay. *From someone else?* Same as above.

KIMMY
47
HIM/HER

I am completely out, but at work I use my birth name and I still dress masculine albeit rocking nail polish because I love my job and love to dress sharp. My coworkers know, my bosses know and I don't experience negativity. I'm sure some people hate me but I generally get along with everybody.

JONATHAN
44
HE/HIM

I never felt that I hid who I was from my family or any employers I have had. I never overly shared who I was but if I was asked I told the truth. I kind of let it come out organically if that makes any kind of sense. Maybe not the best way for dealing but it worked for me at the time.

JV
43
HE/HIM/HIS

I hid it from the family for so long, but now I don't. Whether they like it or not, I am now my own person, and they either love me for who I am or they don't. *From your employer?* No. *From someone else?* It was mostly in college. I was very well known around TX for my dad being a preacher and also I was a singer and sang all over TX in different churches and organizations.

KAYTI
LOOK 32, FEEL 78, LEGALLY 42
RECENTLY FEMALE (SHE/HER/HERS) TO EVERYONE BUT BLOOD FAMILY

Still hiding the magnitude from family, recently came out at work.

RYAN
39
HE/HIM

Growing up in Montana, I think I hid my truth from myself, my family, and my peers. Montana is a very conservative place, and I always felt as if speaking my truth would potentially ruin friendships and relationships, and that it could also potentially threaten my safety.

STEPHEN
38
HE/HIM

Yes, yes, yes.

ANDREW
30
PANSEXUAL TRANSGUY—HE/HIM

To a certain extent I have. I never came out to my elder grandma before she passed. That was partly due to the fact that she passed away before I could but I also didn't ever think to do so before she passed. I also have purposefully never told a few of my coworkers and such to protect myself, when I was able to. I do very much try to pick and choose who I come out to.

JACKSON
30
HE/HIM/HIS

I have tried to hide before, but when your legal name does not match your current identity, it is hard. It always finds a way to reveal itself. I guess my biggest form of trying to hide was being stealthy and staying isolated away from strangers and large crowds. Now I am not so afraid to step out and be social.

MISS JESSICA
27
NON-BINARY, ALL PRONOUNS

Yes, to all of the above.

PARRISH
23
HE/HIM

I have always been myself and I don't think hiding my true self is something I ever did intentionally. I think sometimes people feel that not coming out is equivalent to hiding your true self, which is not entirely the case. In my case, I just didn't fully know or grasp those feelings at the time, so before I came out, I felt that I was my true self until I was at a place to process and understand my feelings for men. Now that I am out, it's just another part of my true self and I hope to find more parts to contribute to the life I am living.

MADI
21
SHE/HER

I spent a summer working at Office Max, and one of my coworkers knew I was gay because she was bi and we had talked about it before, but no one else knew. I remember that I took the weekend of the pride festival off, and when I returned to work on Monday, I over-heard one of the managers talking to another coworker about how he "deserves a straight pride parade if the gays get one." Needless to say, I made sure not to tell him anything about it. He rode his bike to work and drank approximately four Monster Energy drinks in the span of one shift, so naturally his opinion didn't matter much to me, but I did not want to deal with him finding out.

FREYA
20
SHE/HER/HERS

The only time I hide my true self is during work. My family as mentioned is super supportive and never has questioned me. At work, I am much more reserved and afraid to show my true self. I have received backlash and hate for being gay at my workplaces. I don't think it is anyone's business where I work.

***

As is pointed out in one of the answers, people don't necessarily have to hide, they choose to for so many personal reasons. In hindsight, I wish I had phrased the question differently, but I too am always learning. That being said, you can see the difference between the ages. The older people did actually have to hide in order to keep their jobs, but younger people don't have to. But sometimes it is easier that way.

CHAPTER 5

WHAT DO YOU THINK ABOUT ALL OF THE INITIALS FOR THE COMMUNITY, LGBTQ+? DO YOU UNDERSTAND THEM ALL? DO YOU PREFER A DIFFERENT NAME?

CORKY
76
MR.

For so long it was only "LGBT," however the addition of "Q" has been added to "the mix," LOL. Many feel that it is like an umbrella that covers all the other acronyms and an individual can be fluid with their identity and sexuality! During the years of the "millennial generation" growing into adulthood, it didn't seem necessary to label one's self which allowed each person to be changeable, depending on different "factors" of who they are with at any particular time.

DAVID
69
HE

Yes, I understand what the letters mean, but I don't really give a hoot what "we" are called. In this country, I believe the correct term is "human."

JW
66

The initials for the community LGBTQ+ is something that doesn't bother me what it is called. The "+" I'm not sure what that is though. I believe I understand them all but the "+" like I said. I don't have a different name. I haven't even really thought about it.

ROB
66

Drop the Q, especially in this environment.

CJEAN
63
HE/HIM

I want to be inclusive but it gets to be too much. I stop at LGBTQ+. I do know their meanings. I might be convinced to include I (Intersex) and A (Asexual), but the rest are just variations on a theme. There was some comedian that referred to it as alphabet soup which I found funny. I have respect for everyone's orientation.

SHANNON
58

I know that LGBTQ is an important title for many people. I don't really get into labels much. I know what they all mean, it's just not important to me.

TOM
58

It's quite a mouthful. I've never known what "Queer" and "+" in LGBTQ+ mean.

TONY
58
HE/HIM

I have been through so many iterations. At first it was the Gay community, then the Gay and Lesbian community. And then GLBT, but
then it was important to recognize lesbians so they came first. And
then Q+ (or QIA). For some, the experiences are different. E.g., a
transgender person can still be heterosexual, so are the issues the
same? Maybe not, but collectively this speaks to broad marginaliza-
tion based on one's orientation and identity. I don't take issue with
the labeling at all if helps to deepen the conversation and bring similarly marginalized groups together. I regard myself a gay man. I used
to think I was a man, or attorney, or whatever "who happens to be
gay." That "being gay" does not define me. Well, it does. I am a very
out and proud gay man and I don't/won't shy away from the importance of making that distinction.

CHRISTOPHER
57

Yes, I understand the full gamut of LGBTQIA+.

GUS
57
HE/HIM

Honestly, I have always felt a bit uncomfortable with "BTQ+." In a life
where I struggled for so long to understand my own sexual identity,
asking me to fully embrace people who are bisexual, transgendered
or otherwise as "my community" is an honest challenge. It's not
unlike the challenge that I have with some aspects of the gay community (sexual promiscuity or vapid pettiness, for example), with which

I do not feel an affinity. I am me, you be you. We can all celebrate our Pride together for who we are, but that's probably where it ends.

BRAD
54

I'm fine with it. However, we do seem to be getting quite an alphabet going. *Do you understand them all?* Not completely. *Do you prefer a different name?* No.

ANTHONY
53
HE/HIM/HIS

I understand all the initials. I wish we would stop at LGBTQ+, it's very confusing to the general public.

JOHN
52
GAY MALE AND HE/HIM/HIS

I think we should be able to be a more inclusive community without so many dang letters. I personally think it is too many and bordering on dumb.

Do you understand them all? Yes.

Do you prefer a different name? Queer seems like a good all encompassing term but I know I am in a real minority of opinion on all of this. I think all the groups reasonably want distinction and yet they want to be a single banded unit to achieve strength in numbers. Honestly, the needs and desires of each subcommunity rarely align or mutually benefit as much as everyone wants.

And, I am a simplicity oriented person and think if we were all just queer it would help focus the conversations on needs instead of differences.

MIKE
51
HE/HIM/HIS

I think the community has taken it too far. LGBT was enough. I also think adding colors to the rainbow flag misses the symbolism of a rainbow.

PASHA
51
SHE/HER OR THEY/THEM

I normally use "LGBTQIA+" but am not too picky. I sometimes call it the "Alphabet Soup of Love." Some folx get picky about it, but I think there are bigger fish to fry.

DAVID
50
HE/HIM

I'm totally fine with it. It represents everyone. I do understand them all. I always refer to myself as gay or queer.

MICHAEL
50
HE/HIM/HIS

I am fine with them. Every human has a right to be identified and be accounted for.

KIMMY
47
HIM/HER

I know the letters LGBTQ are important. It's needed for representation, especially on a political platform. To ensure rights that weren't clearly stated in the Constitution. I think it's sad though that we feel the need to have labels at the street level. I feel cagey also. I'm now under pressure to choose a letter to represent me. I'm not L. I'm not G. I might be a B because I like Gs and Bs but then I wonder; am I a T because my feminine expressions are as deep as my masculine? That just leaves me with Q. My love hate relationship to the Q word. Queer. One definition of Queer is peculiar. Many feel it is a derogatory slur. Especially if you are 65 or older. I have been made to feel odd or "peculiar" my whole life. Never fitting in. If you are an optimist and peculiar—and one of those "Letters," you could always pass yourself off as artsy if you had to keep it in the closet.

If the legends are true like the Indigenous "Two-Spirited" people from days long past who simply lived either gender and the rest of it's society didn't kill them because it wasn't a big deal, then I want to know when we will be able to go on about our daily lives without having to hear about some unfortunate Johnny Lunchpail who was outed, thrown into their local spotlight and subsequently ruined financially or socially and in many cases got a criminal record. And, that's if Mx Lunchpail is lucky. If they aren't, they are assaulted, raped or killed. Again, I blame the Christians. I know that is not fair but at the time that I was given these questions I have been trying to mend myself, my community, my country and planet by repairing our collective karma one small deed at a time, using my gender-less and gender-full essence that I call me and have come to learn that most of the strife can be attributed to the Christian colonization of the western world. I am renewed with hope however. Looking at our current younger generation, we can see a simple love for each other where there is a sense of coolness, instead of terror when a friend comes out to you. Sure, it's still a letter from the LGBT umbrella but as time goes on maybe the coolness will go away and your friend will just be your friend and not your lesbian friend or gay friend. It seems racist in a way, or discriminatory. I don't say my black friend is meeting me for lunch today. I say my friend is meeting me for lunch.

JONATHAN
44
HE/HIM

I think ALL the initials in LGBTQ+ are great. Whether I understand ALL of them is an entirely different Oprah.

JV
43
HE/HIM/HIS

Because I'm 43, back then I don't really remember having the initials. You were either gay or bi or questioning. Now I love it because so many can identify themselves and feel welcome in our community of inclusion.

KAYTI
LOOK 32, FEEL 78, LEGALLY 42
RECENTLY FEMALE (SHE/HER/HERS) TO EVERYONE BUT BLOOD FAMILY

I prefer the term Queer. It might be owning a derogatory word. I also like kink, but sexuality is not inherently kinky.

What do you think about all of the initials for the community, LGBTQ+?
Do you understand them all? Do you prefer a different name?

RYAN
39
HE/HIM

The LGBTQ+ community initials all have a place at the table. I feel like although the LGBTQ+ community should inherently be a very open and accepting community, there are often people and groups within the community that are still treated in a very marginalized way. Until we welcome everyone to the table, we will never fully actualize our potential and outreach.

STEPHEN
38
HE/HIM

I think I understand what the letters all mean, though I'm always open and interested in learning more. However, I'm personally leaning toward eventually recapturing the term "Queer" to incorporate anyone on the rainbow. I'm not settled on that by any stretch and open to healthy debate on both sides. But, it's a current leaning when asked a preference.

ANDREW
30
PANSEXUAL TRANSGUY—HE/HIM

JACKSON
30
HE/HIM/HIS

I think labels do more damage than good. I think if we all are to see true unity within our society, we cannot isolate any community from one another. Before we are anything, we are HUMAN. I do understand them all and for the purpose of labelling others, I have no qualms or changes suggested.

MISS JESSICA
27
NON-BINARY, ALL PRONOUNS

I understand them all. I think if it makes people feel seen then go for it. I do prefer to use "queer community" as an umbrella term.

PARRISH
23
HE/HIM

I think they are important to be taught in our society. I do not understand them all, but I try to learn more each day. I think gaining an understanding of each initial and identity allows one to become a true ally. I have a difficult time believing someone can be an ally to the LGBTQ+ community if they only focus on one community within it. To be the best ally possible, I think even the smallest understanding of each "subcommunity" is the best valuable asset one can have.

MADI
21
SHE/HER

I think any identity that a person may feel is a valid identity. I have a pretty solid grasp on most of them because I am surrounded by many different people that identify all across the spectrum in college. I personally identify as gay.

What do you think about all of the initials for the community, LGBTQ+?
Do you understand them all? Do you prefer a different name?

FREYA
20
SHE/HER/HERS

I think it's wonderful. I am so glad everyone has their chance to be represented.

***

I love the term used above "alphabet soup of love"! Owning words is important. This is one of those questions where you can definitely see the difference in eras.

CHAPTER 6

HOW DO YOU FEEL ABOUT RELIGION? ARE YOU AT A CHURCH CURRENTLY? HAVE YOU NOT BEEN ACCEPTED?

CORKY
76
MR.

I am very spiritual, but not "religious." I do believe that there is a "Higher Power," but all too often organized religion is more into the structured beliefs of the church and resistant to changing. One prime example, the Christian religion! As with the Catholic religion, changes are coming along in society as a whole, softening their fear and objection to homosexuals! In the 70s, Harvey Milk said, "They (people in general) only have to get to know us"! I am not adverse to going to a church, and be a part of the "collective consciousness" of acceptance, love and peace.

DAVID
69
HE

I taught pre-school Sunday school classes when I was in high school. I seldom had more than a few kids and I'd known each of them since they were born. I know I learned more than they did. Taking Bible stories down to a pre-school level was very instructive. I found so many of these stories far less profound than I had been taught to think they were.

In college, I had a roommate who took several comparative religion classes. I figured if I was ever going to understand anything about religion, the one I was brought up in would be a good place to start. I read several books on early Christianity, including many in the alternate scriptures (I strongly recommend the Nag Hammadi texts). Eventually, I went on to a couple of books on ancient Greek religion (a childhood fascination mainly prompted, I'm sure, by the naked men Greek pottery). Several years ago, I found myself in the British Museum face to face with the Rosetta Stone. I've been dabbling in Egyptian history ever since, especially the evolution of Egyptian religion.

I went to MCC for a while when I lived on Capitol Hill. My mom would call me every Sunday and was always happy if I told her I had gone to church. That lasted until the minister gave a series of sermons on someone's interpretations of the parables. They just got crazier and crazier. I realized that neither the minister nor the person he was parroting knew anything about Mid-Eastern history. Then the guy gave a sermon on the Gnostic Gospels (see the Hag Hammadi texts). It was quickly apparent that I knew infinitely more about them than he did. On the way out of the church, I shook his hand and asked him if he'd read the Gnostics. He turned red in the face and sputtered a "no." That was the last time I went to church for anything other than weddings and funerals with the exception of when I was visiting my parents and would go to church with my mother.

JW
66

My husband and I don't practice any religion, but we both were born in a catholic family environment and attended church on Sundays. I went to a parochial school for the first eight years of my life. We don't have a church we attend now.

ROB
66

I was raised Catholic. Like the Pet Shop Boys explained, everything I do is a sin. I have bitter memories.

CJEAN
63
HE/HIM

I started going to a Missionary Baptist Church at the age of two and never missed a single Sunday service until I was 18. They had pins you wore for continuous attendance and they had a special one for me at 16 years. At 18 when I left home, I stopped cold and never missed going to church again. Even after all the indoctrination, I never really believed it and found most church members racist hypocrites. I have a vivid memory when I was probably eight or nine of a deacon on Easter Sunday, who stopped a lady and her daughter after entering services to walk her out since she was black. I have attended many different religious services out of curiosity—not anything I need other than the sense of community—I can't handle any of the religious doctrines. I always say I was dunked twice (baptism) and officially am only a back slider so really am "saved" just in case.

How do you feel about religion? Are you at a church currently? Have you not been accepted?

SHANNON
58

I grew up in the church. My father was a Southern Baptist pastor, so we were in the church three times a week. As I was dealing with my sexuality, I had a lot of shame. As I studied scripture and commentary, I came to the conclusion that the church was just wrong about their stance on homosexuality. I eventually left the evangelical church and found churches that were open and affirming.

TOM
58

I have positive memories of religion from when I was a child, especially at Christmas. Now, I am not really religious at all. I am a lapsed Catholic. I haven't been to Mass in years, except for weddings and funerals. However, perhaps there is hope for me...I love the Pope. He is so inclusive and human.

TONY
58
HE/HIM

I reject organized religion. I grew up Catholic, but would leave the church after serious exploration. I now identify as atheist. Parents were probably not happy about that. I cannot understand how anyone would want to affiliate with a church that does not accept them in their entirety. "Oh, but I want to change the church!" Yeah, right. I don't see any of my black friends joining the KKK to change it from the inside. Doesn't really work that way. I hold accountable the teachings of so many churches for the suicide rate among the LGBTQ community. It is unforgivable.

CHRISTOPHER
57

As I mentioned early, I grew up catholic, and used to refer to myself as a "recovering catholic." I left the church behind in my late teens, because I could not reconcile myself to a religion that considered me an abomination and I did not believe that a God of love could forsake me for how they made me. I have retained my spirituality throughout my life, I just no longer ascribe to any specific religion.

GUS
57
HE/HIM

After 57 years on this earth, I believe that, on balance, the world would be far better off without religion (John Lennon's *Imagine* may have expressed it best). I grew up in an Uber Catholic home, attended Catholic schools for 12 years, and was an altar boy until I was 18, so I know ALL about "The Church." I don't think that it's being too dramatic to say that it nearly destroyed my life. I realize that not all religions or religious organizations are as nefarious as the Catholic Church, but I have no interest in spending one single moment in one or with one. I also really hate golf.

BRAD
54

I'm spiritual but not religious. Religion has done a disservice to spirituality. My major in college was Religion, Philosophy and Psychology, so don't get me started on the whole religion versus spirituality aspect. *Are you at a church currently?* No, I tried several churches throughout the years and have decided I'm fine with my spirituality.

Have you not been accepted? I was accepted in a couple, but always felt a tad on the outside looking in.

ANTHONY
53
HE/HIM/HIS

I went to a Catholic mass in my younger years. I stopped going to church as they did not accept who I was.

JOHN
52
GAY MALE AND HE/HIM/HIS

I personally identify as Christian but overall am indifferent toward religion. Unfortunately, I see too many people use religion to justify or push discriminatory practices. While I think religion can be great and spirituality can be better, I just don't see enough people practice the good parts enough. Again, good for those who it works for and I hope it leads them to do good deeds.

FWIW I have been through many very spiritual/religious periods of life. Some were part of my hiding but they were always based in wanting to help people and be a better person. When that stopped being the thing I moved away from it.

Are you at a church currently? No. *Have you not been accepted?* N/A

MIKE
51
HE/HIM/HIS

I am spiritual, not religious, and I'm fine with others' beliefs as long as they don't try to impose them on others.

PASHA
51
SHE/HER OR THEY/THEM

I feel that most religions (not just Christian but almost everything including New Age) are designed to project their moral and value system on to others. I was raised in a full gospel church that was beyond homophobic and repressive. I tried to go back to a UCC church but in spite of being "open and affirming," I've never, ever seen them do anything to support LGBTQIA+ or even BIPOC events. Behind the scenes, quite the opposite. So, I left.

DAVID
50
HE/HIM

I am not religious, just spiritual, but I'm respectful of others' beliefs.

MICHAEL
50
HE/HIM/HIS

I am a man of deep faith. I designate as a Born Again Christian, believing that God has created us in his own image. How can I be doing something wrong such as loving another man if God has created me this way. I have accepted Jesus as my Lord and Savior and know I am saved and will go to heaven as he died on the cross to save us all for our sins. *Are you at a church currently?* No. *Have you not been accepted?* Yes, I have.

KIMMY
47
HIM/HER

I went to Catholic school from kindergarten through 3rd grade. I got bullied a lot by the kids on my school bus. I had to wear a suit and tie to school while the public school children got to do whatever they wanted. I was even called a fag and a gaylord before I knew what any of those terms meant. By the time I did know what they meant, I knew enough not to breathe a word of it to anybody. I rejected all Christian philosophies in my 20s. I can't be a member of a supposed divine institution that historically sent people to war all in the name of God and what happens to you when you die. Their stance on LGBT issues speaks for itself as well as their views on women and people of color over the years. I do not believe that the church has changed even though they claim it is evolving. Since then, I have studied many religions and philosophies and no longer need to pursue salvation.

JONATHAN
44
HE/HIM

How do I feel about religion? I don't. I believe that religion is the root of most intolerance and hate both in this country and in the world. I don't begrudge people their religious beliefs but I also believe that you can be a good and moral person without it. Having religion doesn't give anyone any kind of moral superiority. This could stem from me having some negative experiences with the Catholic church. When I see signs like "God Hates Fags" I say to myself, what kind of God, who is supposed to be good and benevolent, would hate anybody? In my mind that is a very spiteful God. I'll sum up what I think about the concept of God and religion in a quote from Lex Luthor:

"If God is all good then he cannot be all powerful. And if God is all powerful then he cannot be all good."

JV
43
HE/HIM/HIS

I don't practice anymore. But I still pray and have faith in God. He's gotten me through so much, and so many people I know aren't believers and that's okay. I feel like they still see the light in me. *Are you at a church currently?* No. *Have you not been accepted?* I don't go to church when home, usually because I know I'm not truly accepted.

KAYTI
LOOK 32, FEEL 78, LEGALLY 42
RECENTLY FEMALE (SHE/HER/HERS) TO EVERYONE BUT BLOOD FAMILY

4th generation raised in the same church, was nearly a youth minister 20 years ago. Not actively practicing, not accepted and was outed in a youth group by a "trusted" friend once.

RYAN
39
HE/HIM

My faith is actually what carried me through the darkest times of my coming out period. It has been my source of strength and hope, and it is very important to me. However, I find organized religion to often be a breeding ground for words and actions that can ostracize and cut down members of the LGBTQ+ community. So, I do not find myself feeling a need to be in a church setting regularly.

STEPHEN
38
HE/HIM

Definitely a loaded and nuanced question and answer for me. I grew up Catholic, converted and was baptized again at age 19 in the Evangelical Protestant church, non-denominational affiliation. I was very active as a worship leader, Bible group member and house study host. I also spent some time supervising graduate counseling students at a seminary for a year. Since my marriage and eventual divorce and coming fully out as gay brought me to a place of questioning pretty much everything I've been raised to believe, I've taken a significant step back from any religious affiliation or involvement. I don't consider myself a Christian anymore, nor do I have much of a spiritual life. I am, however, fully aware that much of that step-back is a product of my recent experiences and likely a bit of a pendulum swing that will eventually swing back to some degree of spiritual acceptance and relationship with my higher power. I haven't a clue what that might look like, but I'm open to that happening organically as feels authentic and true for me.

ANDREW
30
PANSEXUAL TRANSGUY—HE/HIM

I am generally neutral about religion. I've seen it be both a positive and a negative presence in people's lives, both in those I know personally and in a more general manner. I think it's something that if it is good for you, keep it; if it's not, dump it so to speak.

I grew up in a secular Christian home. My dad's side of the family is Catholic, while my mom's side of the family is Presbyterian. With this, I grew up rarely going to church of any kind outside of weddings and funerals. I did grow up celebrating Christmas and Easter, just in a not so religious fashion. As an adult, I've contemplated finding/ going to church, in search of community more than anything.

JACKSON
30
HE/HIM/HIS

I was born into religion; however, as I have matured, I grasp onto spirituality more. I cannot deny that a lot of my experiences and schools of thought came from religious principles. I am not currently a member of any church, but my mother is and always will be my spiritual advisor.

MISS JESSICA
27
NON-BINARY, ALL PRONOUNS

I grew up catholic. I consider myself a spiritual person in the sense of the universe and energy working together to create life's experience. I feel indifferent about it until someone tries to use it as a weapon against me.

PARRISH
23
HE/HIM

I have a very difficult time with religion. I just have never under-stood how a superior being could preach acceptance, but then the community following that, turns around and throws hatred toward people. Even more so, in the case of the LGBTQ+ community. I have started to be more open to the idea of religion through conversations with my father about how religion and faith are two different things. Religion is interpreted and things get lost through interpretation.

Faith is one's own understanding and life through religion. I don't think I am describing this the best, but my faith is different than someone else's faith.

MADI
21
SHE/HER

Personally, I believe that religion is a coping mechanism that humans created in order to deal with grief. I don't necessarily have an issue with that, but I do have an issue with what religion has morphed into. It has become the backboard for people to discriminate against the LGBTQ+ community because of their "religious freedom" rights. It makes me infuriated that that is even acceptable in modern society, but here we are. I grew up attending a very accepting and open church, and I enjoy the connections I have made through the church. I enjoy the time I've spent there, but personally, I am not religious in the slightest and don't practice anything. I do believe in an afterlife, but not in the sense of heaven or hell.

FREYA
20
SHE/HER/HERS

I am a very open person. I do not follow a religion or a church, however I am open to others' ideas.

***

Religion seems to be the catalyst for intolerance which makes me sad, especially when I was taught about Jesus accepting everyone with love and openness.

71

CHAPTER 7

HAVE YOU EXPERIENCED CONVERSION THERAPY? DESCRIBE YOUR EXPERIENCE.

CORKY
76
MR.

No, I have not experienced "Conversion Therapy" and am so happy that 25 states have now banned it in their state!

DAVID
69
HE

In college, I went to a shrink that tried to convince me I could develop an interest in women by jacking off looking at girly magazines. I think I saw her twice.

JW
66

No conversion therapy. No experiences.

ROB
66

No. Hell no. But I think my parents thought I had mental problems and shipped me off to stay with my sister in Miami for six months. Like warm air would cure something inside me.

CJEAN
63
HE/HIM

Luckily, no.

SHANNON
58

No conversion therapy. I saw a therapist for about a year to help me accept my sexuality.

TOM
58

I never had to endure that ordeal.

TONY
58
HE/HIM

Nope. It is nothing short of criminal.

CHRISTOPHER
57

I have never experienced "conversion therapy," but I am aware of many of the associated horror stories, up to and including, suicides that were as a result of it.

GUS
57
HE/HIM

No. However, I have experienced the pre-emptive version of conversion therapy, which may be even more prevalent. From a young age, gay people were vilified as sinners of the highest order. For me, having an older gay brother who was in the theatre gave my parents the perfect scapegoat for how gay people are "different and unhappy." Ironically, they really leveraged his fame with their Broadway loving friends.

BRAD
54

No, thank God.

ANTHONY
53
HE/HIM/HIS

No.

JOHN
52
GAY MALE AND HE/HIM/HIS

No.

MIKE
51
HE/HIM/HIS

No.

PASHA
51
SHE/HER OR THEY/THEM

I had to experience, "Deliverance Ministry," during which all kinds of demons were cast out of me. I was sexually assaulted during the process of, "casting out the demon of lust," so obviously, it wasn't great.

DAVID
50
HE/HIM

I have not but [my partner] has.

MICHAEL
50
HE/HIM/HIS

No, although my religious father thought it to be something that could potentially work.

KIMMY
47
HIM/HE

I have never considered conversion therapy. I would have killed myself if I was outed and forced by my family to go.

JONATHAN
44
HE/HIM

Thankfully, I have not experienced conversion therapy.

JV
43
HE/HIM/HIS

NO.

KAYTI
LOOK 32, FEEL 78, LEGALLY 42
*RECENTLY FEMALE (SHE/HER/HERS) TO EVERYONE BUT
BLOOD FAMILY*

Not knowingly—I did a lot of therapy between ages 6-14.

RYAN
39
HE/HIM

I have not.

STEPHEN
38
HE/HIM

Yes, I attended a week-long conversion therapy experience down in Houston back in 2015. It was there I met the man who had created these intensives over 20 years previously. After attending the week and then flying back to Denver, I called him up and asked him to continue as my personal therapist. I saw him for weekly therapy for another year. During this time, my anxiety grew significantly to the point of diagnosable (I'm a licensed therapist myself), which, in turn, eventually bled over into clinical depression. He was actually appropriately empathetic and reflected back that our work was clearly not working and that I was going backward. He eventually challenged me to have a more direct serious talk with my wife about my mental health and making some significant changes in our relationship (she had known about my "struggle" since we'd started dating). We agreed to stop being sexual but just focus on continued building of intimacy, emotional and physical in other ways. I tried this intently for another year or so until my anxiety and depression were so bad I couldn't function much but go to work and come home, and even that was a struggle most days. I eventually started seeing another therapist who helped me more directly face my truth and accept it and begin to have more honest conversations with my wife about what, if any future we could have. I would soon after ask for the divorce.

ANDREW
30
PANSEXUAL TRANSGUY—HE/HIM

I've been fortunate to not!

JACKSON
30
HE/HIM/HIS

I never experienced conversion therapy, but I did grow up in Bible belt south, with a deeply religious family.

MISS JESSICA
27
NON-BINARY, ALL PRONOUNS

I am thankful that I have not.

PARRISH
23
HE/HIM

I have not.

MADI
21
SHE/HER

I have not experienced conversion therapy thankfully. It is despicable.

FREYA
20
SHE/HER/HERS

I have never experienced conversion therapy.

***

Conversion therapy is a horrible thing and I am happy that not many of these people have had to experience it. The fact that conversion therapy even exists is, in my opinion, horrible! I have Pollyanna hopes that this kind of "therapy" goes away completely because the damage it does is awful.

CHAPTER 8

HAVE YOU EXPERIENCED ABUSE AND/OR BIGOTRY? WHAT HAPPENED?

CORKY
76
MR.

Luckily, I've never experienced abuse or bigotry personally...not too many can say that. LOL. When I was in school (1st grade through high school graduation) there wasn't nearly the epidemic or "bullying" that is prevalent these days. If there had been, I may well have been a "perfect target," but I was able to "get along" with everyone, so I've never encountered either.

DAVID
69
HE

Who hasn't? I got slugged in the face a couple of times in high school and called a sissy (which I was, and definitely not one of the jocks).

Twenty or so years ago I had surgery. A few weeks later, I was at a gay bar and a dose of the anesthesia kicked out of my liver (a fact I learned later) and I couldn't keep my eyes open. I had one beer, so

I went to my car to try to wake up. All of a sudden, there were three or four police cars in the parking lot and an officer was ordering me out of the car. I told him I was in my car (keys out of the ignition) because I couldn't stay awake but I wasn't drunk. I got hauled to the drunk tank anyway. When they took a blood test, they asked me if I could get a ride home because I was sober.

One of my favorite harassments was in New Albany, Indiana. I'd gone to the river walk and ran into a very talkative gay man. As we were talking, a car drove by and yelled "faggots." Without skipping a beat the guy yelled, at the top of his lungs, "So good of you to remember!"

I've been called "faggot" and "queer" more times than I can count, but since then I just remember New Albany even if I don't respond.

JW
66

Just bullied in my younger years. Not necessarily gay, but being called a queer.

ROB
66

I was roughed up and humiliated in high school. I was in advanced classes as a freshman and sophomore; older boys would throw books at my head. They broke every window in my car. I was beat up badly when I was 40 near a gay bar by four attackers. They left me on the ground and as they drove away yelled, "Next time you die, faggot." The repeated blows loosened many teeth, leading to 20+ years of infection and loss.

CJEAN
63
HE/HIM

I have been lucky that I have not been attacked or seriously bullied, just excluded at times.

SHANNON
58

I haven't experienced overt bigotry. Just subtle. No abuse.

TOM
58

Never.

TONY
58
HE/HIM

Oh, the list is too long. I have been called "faggot" more times than I can count. I have been physically assaulted. I have been publicly rejected and made fun of by co-workers. Of course, most of this occurred many, many years ago. Certainly this is not the experience of today, but I also choose to live in communities where being openly gay is not an issue.

CHRISTOPHER
57

Abuse and bigotry were part and parcel of being gay in the 70s, 80s and really, up until fairly recently. Very rarely did it involve physical abuse, although that did happen. Having military experience gave me some skills at self defense, though they weren't needed often. My verbal skills with humor and sarcasm were generally most effective at deterring would-be bullies.

GUS
57
HE/HIM

Other than the aforementioned Catholic childhood, I haven't experienced direct abuse or bigotry. I'd imagine that I may have experienced some workplace bigotry in the corporate world, but I worked hard to circumvent that and have had the last laugh.

BRAD
54

Not abuse, but a little bigotry from time to time. Especially in the South. *What happened?* I've been called "faggot" several times while running/jogging in public, had a bottle thrown at my car one night in Dallas—mostly in the 80s and 90s.

ANTHONY
53
HE/HIM/HIS

No.

JOHN
52
GAY MALE AND HE/HIM/HIS

A cab driver verbally assaulted my boyfriend (now husband) and I for kissing in his cab once. When I demanded to be let out, he locked us in because I refused to pay. There was alcohol involved and it escalated to a point the police had to be involved. Honestly, I overreacted and the whole experience put a horrible end to what had a been a great date/celebratory night for us. But, it was the most blunt discrimination I had experienced to date and it was very upsetting to say the least.

Then, of course, the entire gay population of the USA experienced it under the Reagans when they basically said let them die. I mean, look at the way they treated their "friend," Rock Hudson. Deplorable and certainly in hindsight blatant bigotry toward an entire part of the populace.

MIKE
51
HE/HIM/HIS

Many times, particularly in high school. I was taunted, threatened, punched and had a cigarette put out on the back of my neck.

PASHA
51
SHE/HER OR THEY/THEM

Being a foreign born BIPOC, single mother who is queer, hatred baked into every facet of society in rural Oklahoma, and it is part of the reason I left. Things are better here as far as on the surface. However, even in our own community, I see liberal LGBTQIA+ peers pick and choose. We've had many staunch volunteers who signed on to support kids at LGBTQIA+ events that have made it clear through (lack) of action and conversations that supporting BIPOC events is not what they signed on for and that, "those people," should defend their own, basically, and that we are losing focus by going to those rallies and marches.

DAVID
50
HE/HIM

Yes, I used to all the time. I was bullied from junior high into high school and even beyond. I was called faggot daily, hit, spit on, pushed, beaten up and so on. Even got hit over the head with a sawed off wooden hammer handle.

MICHAEL
50
HE/HIM/HIS

Not in a harsh, specific manner but bigotry in general, yes.

KIMMY
47
HIM/HER

JONATHAN
44
HE/HIM

I have been fortunate not to have experienced abuse or much bigotry. The one instance I can think of is when my friends and I were celebrating my 30th birthday in Chicago. We were heading to dinner and a, I think, homeless person harassed us by yelling that we could keep on "swishing" down the street even though we would find "no gay bars that way."

JV
43
HE/HIM/HIS

Not a whole lot. I had an ex that was abusive, mostly from drugs. *What happened?* It took one time and I said goodbye for ever.

KAYTI
LOOK 32, FEEL 78, LEGALLY 42
RECENTLY FEMALE (SHE/HER/HERS) TO EVERYONE BUT BLOOD FAMILY

Emotional abuse is a staple in my life.

RYAN
39
HE/HIM

I have been threatened and called inappropriate names for merely walking across the street (most often while I was living in Montana). Fortunately, I feel that the world has progressed a bit in the past 20 years. Yet, our current political climate threatens to welcome those actions back into mainstream behavior.

STEPHEN
38
HE/HIM

I was molested when I was four years old by my babysitter's 14-year-old son. I was then molested again when I was 15 by a senior in high school while we were away at summer church camp. I was certainly bullied throughout high school with many people assuming I was gay. With years of therapy, I've worked through a great deal of the molestations and the bullying. I am still in therapy for the bullying as it's by far the hardest trauma from my past.

ANDREW
30
PANSEXUAL TRANSGUY—HE/HIM

I've been relatively lucky in this regard that I've only dealt with minor incidents. I experienced a bunch of bias at the job I was working at soon after college. I had a handful of people who were supportive of my identity and transition, but I also had a handful of people who struggled to accept and support me. For example, one of the bosses wouldn't make sure my chosen name was on the schedules, but one of his assistants made a point to go in after and change it for me. This was all before I legally got my name changed. I had a few other coworkers who would make inappropriate remarks semi-regularly to both me directly and to other coworkers.

JACKSON
30
HE/HIM/HIS

I live in America during 2021, it is hard to not experience some form of bigotry. We still are an oppressed people even from a progressive point of view.

MISS JESSICA
27
NON-BINARY, ALL PRONOUNS

I have verbally. I am thankful that nothing has happened to me yet that has been so extreme. I am a thick skin fighter and refuse to let the best be gotten of me.

PARRISH
23
HE/HIM

I have been called derogatory names, to which I just brush off.

MADI
21
SHE/HER

I spent my first semester of college at ASU, and planned to transfer back home to UNC for a variety of reasons. When I made the transfer, I was assigned to a roommate in the dorms. She was very kind when we first started talking and planning about what we would each bring. I knew that I should probably tell her that I had a girlfriend that would be visiting every once in a while, so I sent her a text about it. Her demeanor immediately changed, and she texted me back saying that it wasn't okay, and she "would not be comfortable rooming with a gay person." This was very painful for me. I remember I was out bowling with some friends when she texted me that, and I immediately went to the bathroom crying. My friend came to comfort me, and I showed her the text. She was livid, and was a huge support to me while I tried to find a new roommate. My dad called UNC in the morning to ask what we should do, and the woman on the phone was both shocked and angry that this had happened to me. She apologized profusely and ended up finding me a roommate who had two moms and was very accepting of me. I was very impressed with her swift reaction and action. I ended up getting along great with my new roommate. I used to walk past the room I was supposed to be in while I went to my friend's room, and I always looked for the girl, but I never saw her.

87

FREYA
20
SHE/HER/HERS

Unfortunately, yes. I have received a lot of harassment in terms of my previous workplaces. I have been harassed by many men and cat-called quite a few times for being around my significant other.

***

These answers brought tears to my eyes. Nobody should have to experience these things. Abuse and bigotry are unacceptable, ALWAYS! Being both white and hetero, I work every day to use the voice that I have to stop all of this. And I hope that educating and sharing the experiences will make abusers/bullies think and hopefully stop. So much better than it used to be, but still so much work to be done.

CHAPTER 9

WHAT IS THE GREATEST CHANGE FOR THE COMMUNITY YOU'VE SEEN IN YOUR LIFETIME?

CORKY
76
MR.

When you've been in the "Gay Scene" for as long as I have, you've seen the difference like "night and day"! When I was first coming to terms with myself, that I was "officially gay," it was necessary to "sneak" into gay bars that were "hidden," off the beaten path! As an 18 year old, I did find out where there was one, but going to it presented a huge problem for me. LOL! In 1968 (before 16th Street Mall), the Friday—Saturday night "routine" was for the "older teens" from the entire metropolitan area to cruise down 16th to (about) Curtis, go to 15th and make the loop again...so many that you'd only go about a block every 10ish minutes. LOL. This was great for all those straight kids, but the gay bar was right in "line" of their driving! Before the Denver Pavilions, there was a movie theater, Denver Theater, directly across 16th from the Paramount Theater. My dilemma was the bar was in an alley right next to the Denver Theater. I would have to get to the corner of Glenarm and 16th, then go as fast as I could into the alley...always afraid that my brother, his friends, my high school friends or anyone who knew me wouldn't be driving by at that moment! The age to be in bars was 21, but I'd just hang out by the door until somebody would say, "Come on in Baby" :-)! It certainly wasn't easy, yet when I did get it, there was a "sense of safety, love and belonging!

Now fast forward to '70. Denver had improved, we now had three bars, but still "boring," so a friend and I moved to San Francisco! I had signed a contract to teach that year, so off we went in June. OMG, it was like we had found "Nirvana" with such "freedom" to be yourself without fear of reproach in living or work environments! We didn't know (at that time) the same change was happening in NYC. Stonewall opened up a whole new world for GLBT people! Ironically, I could have stayed in Denver and the "change" would have come to me. Coming back to visit in '73, we were amazed to find a "growing gay community" with more bars, including dance bars! Even so, I was fortunate to be in San Francisco during "The Harvey Milk Days." When I returned to Denver in '83, the societal changes were happening rapidly and continued to the place of respect and prominence we enjoy today. Harvey Milk said it way back in '75, "They only have to get to know us." :-D!

DAVID
69
HE

I read about the Stonewall riots in an underground newspaper when I was in college. I have seen so many changes since then. Mayor Pete as Secretary of Transportation has to be the ultimate change.

JW
66

Being accepted.

ROB
66

Greater acceptance and allegiance with the rest of society. I never thought I'd live long enough to see marriage equality.

CJEAN
63
HE/HIM

The AIDS crisis taking so many of us too soon. We will always be missing almost an entire generation of contributions to our world. I feel gay people have always contributed more than their share since we have been excluded from so much.

SHANNON
58

I have seen huge changes in the community over the years. I used to be afraid that if people knew I was gay, they may try to kill me and that my family would disown me. I never thought I would be married to a woman I loved and never thought I would have children. Truly, the first big change I saw toward acceptance of gay people is when Ellen came out. She did a great deal to normalize homosexuality. I have seen a huge change in mainline churches and society in general. I live openly at work, in my neighborhood and at church. I never dreamed I would live the life I live. Colorado is not as open as the East coast. People aren't as accustomed to seeing families like ours. Everything is subtle. Example: when I met my dentist the first time, he flinched when I mentioned my wife. These things happen often and are uncomfortable, but are a long ways from the "Matthew Shepherd" days.

TOM
58

Increased acceptance into society at large.

TONY
58
HE/HIM

Where to begin. The definition of privilege is never having the Supreme Court decide your rights. Well, in my adult lifetime alone, the Supreme Court has weighed in on whether cities and states can pass anti-discrimination laws protecting the LGBTQ community (Romer versus Evans), whether gay sex can be criminalized (Lawrence versus Texas), and gay marriage (Windsor followed by Obergefell).

But I must admit, I wasn't sure I would see marriage in my lifetime. It seems weird to say that out loud now, but it has only been the law of the land for five years. So, let me back up a bit and tell you a bit more about myself.

I mentioned that my friends teased that I stormed out of the closet and right out the front door. I had always been interested in politics and the law and I knew there were fights going on all over the country (Boulder at the time, too) to protect the rights of lesbians and gays in employment, housing, etc. After a bit of research, I discovered that Denver (my home city) did not have any anti-discrimination ordinance of any kind. With a friend, I formed the Equal Protection Ordinance Coalition and we drafted a comprehensive anti-discrimination ordinance for Denver and spent nearly two years building an incredible coalition to get it passed by city council. Our sponsor and collaborator was Kathy Reynolds (who recently passed). From that point, a group of idiots sought to overturn the "sexual orientation" portion of the law alone. I co-chaired the campaign to defeat the attempted repeal in what was known as Initiated Ordinance No. 1. We successfully fought back the attempted repeal, but the right wing came after the community with Amendment Two, which would pass in 1996 and would give rise to the Supreme Court case of Romer versus Evans. I could go on forever, but will just leave things here.

CHRISTOPHER
57

The greatest change I've seen in my lifetime? Wow. Well, although I was too young to know about it at the time, I was around for Stonewall, the beginning of all that has come about since. I came of age during the age of AIDS, and lived with the visceral dread that came with it. I buried probably 100 or more friends, including my first love before I turned 30. I saw the advent of "don't ask, don't tell," I marched with Act Up against the genocide of watching so much of my generation perish because as long as AIDS killed only gay men, it was not a high research priority. I fought back against the inherently unequal status of "civil unions" and got to watch with triumph as Obergefell versus Hodges became the law of the land. It has been a long road, and the costs were great, but worth it if a future young person's greatest concern is what matching tuxedos they and their date will wear to prom.

GUS
57
HE/HIM

When I was younger, probably up to the beginning of the 2nd Obama administration, our "community" was on the fringe of society. In the period from 2010—2016 something magical happened. Suddenly, we were a political force, the "kids" didn't seem to think much of their friends coming out, and we were more and more prevalent on TV and in movies. For me, the single greatest change was the Supreme Court ruling on marriage equality and the increasing public face and acceptance of same sex families.

BRAD
54

Marriage equality. Never saw that coming. I thought I'd die before that happened.

ANTHONY
53
HE/HIM/HIS

Just how visible we are and that we can publicly share who we love.

JOHN
52
GAY MALE AND HE/HIM/HIS

Marriage Equality.

MIKE
51
HE/HIM/HIS

Marriage equality.

PASHA
51
SHE/HER OR THEY/THEM

Definitely getting the right to legally marry has been the hugest accomplishment within my lifetime. However, I still see us all fighting for basic human rights and acceptance that we've been struggling for decades and we're still spinning our wheels.

DAVID
50
HE/HIM

That more people are open and accepting about it. Businesses and stores promoting safe places for LGBTQ+.

MICHAEL
50
HE/HIM/HIS

The fact that I can openly, in the workplace or on the street, in public or in my own home, in church and before God, profess my love for another man. I never thought that this day would come. Although there is so much hatred and bigotry in our country and there will never be ultimate acceptance, I feel there have been major strides.

KIMMY
47
HIM/HER

Visibility. I am filled with hope when I see the younger generation express themselves fearlessly. I'm also thrilled people have the right to be married if they choose.

JONATHAN
44
HE/HIM

The greatest change bar none is just the visibility of the community. When you think back in our history when people would have to hide and/or go underground just to express who they were and be with who they loved, the progress is amazing. Not to mention the progress we have made in our portrayals in movies and television. If you have ever seen the original 1970 version of *The Boys in the Band*, you'll see exactly what I'm talking about.

JV
43
HE/HIM/HIS

Just how inclusive our community is now mostly. But how it's really so much easier in a way for others to come out and not feel alone. Even though some still do.

KAYTI
LOOK 32, FEEL 78, LEGALLY 42
RECENTLY FEMALE (SHE/HER/HERS) TO EVERYONE BUT BLOOD FAMILY

Improved optics in the media.

RYAN
39
HE/HIM

Marriage equality has been the greatest change and accomplishment that I have seen in the past decade that gives me great hope for our community.

STEPHEN
38
HE/HIM

Acceptance from so many that being gay isn't a sin, mental illness, wrong.

ANDREW
30
PANSEXUAL TRANSGUY—HE/HIM

I've seen the continual visible presence of the LGBTQ+ community in the media, starting (for me at least, in my lifetime) with Ellen on her show in 1997. Allowing more people to be accepting and for others to come out, both publicly and/or on a personal level.

JACKSON
30
HE/HIM/HIS

The greatest change for the community I have seen in my lifetime would be the legalization of gay marriage federally. That was something my wife and I struggled with before my transition.

MISS JESSICA
27
NON-BINARY, ALL PRONOUNS

The greatest change that I've personally seen is marriage equality. Mixed with drag becoming a mainstream for EVERYONE.

PARRISH
23
HE/HIM

I remember when gay marriage was legalized and a part of me jumped for joy before I was even out. I truly don't know if it was my own deep excitement popping out, or for my friends I saw celebrating.

MADI
21
SHE/HER

The biggest change I have seen in my lifetime was the legalization of gay marriage in the US. I was abroad in Holland at a student conference when it was legalized. I remember that they were in the middle of two presentations, and a woman came on stage to announce the breaking news. The crowd started clapping and cheering, and it was a very hopeful moment for me to experience. I was only out to my friend Sophie and my family at this time, so internally I was screaming cries of joy, but externally I tried to play it off like it was exciting, but not *too* exciting.

FREYA
20
SHE/HER/HERS

I think I have seen more love and acceptance from outside the community. There are plenty of people who do not identify within the LGBTQ+ but I have seen more love and acceptance from those outside of the community.

***

I remember in high school being in the inner circle of a couple of friends who were out but only to a few of us. Now I see high schoolers going to prom with whoever they want—acceptance and visibility strides! Being the mom of a gay daughter, I cried tears of joy when marriage equality passed because it was one less obstacle she would have to hurdle, and joy that everyone could openly express their love!

CHAPTER 10

WHAT IS THE ONE WORD PERTAINING TO LGBTQ+ PEOPLE YOU CAN'T STAND? FAVORITE WORD?

CORKY
76
MR.

I have no problem with any of the words associated with our LGBTQ+ community.

DAVID
69
HE

I don't know that there are many that I can't stand. The first time I was referred to as "she," I was offended but as soon as I got my dander up, I realized that being seen as effeminate had been one of my greatest fears. Then I realized I no longer cared. The first touts of "faggot" or "queer" stung a little but, to paraphrase, I thought "but you are Blanch!" I stopped worrying about such applets after that.

JW
66

ROB
66

I loathe the word faggot. I like "gurl."

CJEAN
63
HE/HIM

1) Assimilation or Integration. I mourn the loss of a distinct gay culture. Unfortunately, as we become more accepted into "regular" society, our uniqueness becomes less and less. There was something enticing about being outside the norm, making your own rules of behavior, not in the binary-hetero-normative.

2) Lifestyle—it's a life, not a lifestyle.

Favorite: Camp, Pride, Drag.

SHANNON
58

Faggot or Dyke. Though it is perfectly acceptable for us to call each other this.

TOM
58

I can't stand the word "queeny." My favorite word is "equality."

TONY
58
HE/HIM

Not sure what you are looking for here. I am reminded of Joe Jackson's lyric, "Don't call me faggot unless you are my friend." One of the greatest strengths of our community is its diversity. Taking back the power of the language has been important to building our collective strength.

CHRISTOPHER
57

I am okay with the whole lexicon that is LGBTQAI+. I don't have a favorite per se.

GUS
57
HE/HIM

Don't like: Faggot
Favorite: Pride

BRAD
54

Faggot is one I can't stand. Queer is my favorite—I feel it embraces the entire community, not just gay/lesbian people.

ANTHONY
53
HE/HIM/HIS

Faggot. Don't believe I have a favorite word.

11

JOHN
52
GAY MALE AND HE/HIM/HIS

MIKE
51
HE/HIM/HIS

Faggot and no favorite.

PASHA
51
SHE/HER OR THEY/THEM

I still dislike the word, "faggot." I love the word, "normalization." To me, the best word is when there isn't a requirement for one at all. When being LGBTQIA+ is such a non-issue, it isn't even necessary to acknowledge anything.

DAVID
50
HE/HIM

I used to hate faggot but now it makes me laugh for some reason. And my favorite is gay or queer and of course fabulous! LOL!

MICHAEL
50
HE/HIM/HIS

N/A

KIMMY
47
HIM/HER

JONATHAN
44
HE/HIM

I'm just going to say it. Queer. Queer is the one word I still have a problem with when it comes to the LGBTQ+ community. I know, I know, what about the f-word? Yes, that's horrible as well, but the word queer still rankles me even as the younger members of our community are taking the word back. I'm just not there with the word queer yet.

JV
43
HE/HIM/HIS

I love QUEEN? Hah!

KAYTI
LOOK 32, FEEL 78, LEGALLY 42
RECENTLY FEMALE (SHE/HER/HERS) TO EVERYONE BUT BLOOD FAMILY

Pass.

RYAN
39
HE/HIM

I hate the word "Fem." I find it derogatory, and it just grates on me. I love the word "Dorothy"!

STEPHEN
38
HE/HIM

ANDREW
30
PANSEXUAL TRANSGUY—HE/HIM

I don't personally have any one word that bugs me more then any others or that I favor over any others either.

JACKSON
30
HE/HIM/HIS

One word pertaining to LGBTQ+ people I can't stand is "dyke or faggot." I find them terribly offensive.

MISS JESSICA
27
NON-BINARY, ALL PRONOUNS

I personally don't like the use of "Faggot" in anyway, however it doesn't bother me when queer people use it in a "take back" way. My favorite word is "Queer."

PARRISH
23
HE/HIM

MADI
21
SHE/HER

I get extremely annoyed when people refer to my girlfriend as my "partner." I completely understand the importance of the word partner, as it is important to non-binary or gender nonconforming relationships, but I can't stand when people say that about my personal relationship, as my girlfriend and I both identify as female. When talking about a straight couple, you don't say "partner," you say girlfriend or boyfriend. My relationship is no different to theirs, and it is almost degrading to me when people say "partner" instead of girlfriend because it makes it sound illegitimate to me.

FREYA
20
SHE/HER/HERS

I do not like the word lesbian at all. I think it is a weird word and I just do not like it. Favorite word I guess would be gay just because that is how I identify.

***

The f-word!

I like the word "human."

CHAPTER 11

HOW HAS AIDS/HIV IMPACTED YOU?

CORKY
76
MR.

Once again, I have been so fortunate. My last years in San Francisco '81—June, '83, before anyone knew what was killing gay men, I was a SF street artist, so I spent (almost) 24/7 making my craft, then going to Fisherman's Wharf to make my living! TG I was in no way "promiscuous" like so many, at that time and in that city! The disease was rampant, but the first person I "directly" knew who died from it was a Denver friend who chose not to move to SF with us in 1970. He passed shortly after I moved back. Again, as luck would have it, even after returning I didn't go out to be a part of "Denver's Gay Community." Learning of Scott contacting and dying of AIDS I totally devoted my time, for 16 more years, to my family's day care center, my mom and our home.

DAVID
69
HE

I've lost so many friends, starting with my best friend from college early in the plague. The loss of friends and confidants has probably been the most profound change the plague has made in my life. All my gay friends from college are gone as are so many of my friends from the 70s and 80s too.

JW
66

What affected me was seeing the guys getting sick and dying. Not anyone I had hung out with, but reading and seeing men get sick and dying.

ROB
66

Fortunately, David and I were already together when the crisis hit. It was devastating to watch so many friends die. I've never recovered from that.

CJEAN
63
HE/HIM

I lost almost everyone I knew in the 80s—to this day I still cry over that void left in my life. I have never been tested for the gene but am convinced I am unable to acquire HIV genetically. There is absolutely no reason why I should not be positive, but yet I am not. I still practice a safer sex life.

SHANNON
58

I personally haven't been affected by HIV/AIDS.

TOM
58

My cousin died of AIDS many years ago. It was a long, drawn-out, painful, awful decline to death. Such a tragic waste of a very nice man. He was always my favorite cousin when I was growing up.

TONY
58
HE/HIM

Wow, another doozy of a question. I could go on for pages on this topic alone. Recall I came out in the late 80s when AIDS was really becoming a thing. I am going to short circuit this a bit. I lost too many friends. Actually had to stop going to funerals. Visits to hospice were a regular thing. In the course of 18 months, I lost more than a dozen friends—not just acquaintances. It was a very painful time. I was involved with ACT UP Denver for some time, picketing the mayor and governor, die-in at the Department of Health. And then got involved on a task force with Governor Romer and Lt. Governor Callahan. I even took on former Governor Lamm during a course he was teaching at Denver University, as he publicly opposed funding for certain AIDS treatments "as they are going to die anyway." You might recall that Lamm promoted the "duty to die" for the elderly.

My dad was wrong, I never got "burned" by AIDS ... I remain negative today. But when I think of the countless lives lost due to inaction by a feckless president (Reagan), and lackluster health departments, it makes me seethe. I am so grateful for the medical advances as I have many friends who are positive (and undetectable) and living full and complete lives.

One of the untold stories about the impact of HIV/AIDS on the gay community is the often unrecognized contribution of the lesbian community during that time. The gay community owes so much to the lesbians who became caregivers and were some of the loudest voices in the fights to bring attention to and combat the disease.

COVID has certainly brought back so many memories of this time.

CHRISTOPHER
57

See #9.

GUS
57
HE/HIM

It killed my beloved older brother and best buddy. I was 29, he was 42, and my life was never quite the same. I still cry thinking about him, as I am now. He was a smart, handsome, athletic, talented and very funny man who loved his little brother like no one else. He accomplished more in his short life than most people in a lifetime. AIDS sucks.

BRAD
54

My late husband, Chris, was a nurse and was one of the first home health nurses in Dallas to help HIV/AIDS people. Other home health nurses would not go to their homes to draw blood, administer meds, etc. He was recognized as one of Dallas's Great 100 Nurses in the 90s for his contribution to the HIV community. We saw hundreds of people get sick and many died. The church we attended at the time had a day of recognition for those that passed away from AIDS, and we would always lose count of the people we knew or Chris had taken care of during his nursing days. It was a terribly difficult time in the Dallas gay community, and I'm so thankful that medical advances have helped people live longer with AIDS now.

ANTHONY
53
HE/HIM/HIS

I'm HIV negative which I'm extremely grateful for since I came out in the mid 80s. I haven't lost many close friends to the disease though I know several who are HIV positive and have amazing lives.

JOHN
52
GAY MALE AND HE/HIM/HIS

I came of age sexually as the AIDS pandemic was ravaging the gay communities across the US and world. It terrified me of sex and certainly did a lot to emotionally keep me in the closet TBH. My aunt worked in the PR department of the CDC in Atlanta, so I had a front row depiction of all the bad that was happening. Just imagine, 18-year-old male horniness with the world view of sex kills, I can't be that. It was honestly awful.

It took me until my 30s to truly understand so much about HIV and AIDS and medical science and respecting people who were infected. AIDS and HIV have been a central part of my gay experience despite the fact that I am HIV negative. As such, this has also pushed me to become educated and to educate others and has had a lot to do with our desire to participate in the AIDS/Lifecycle twice to date.

MIKE
51
HE/HIM/HIS

I lost several friends.

PASHA
51
SHE/HER OR THEY/THEM

Growing up in the 80s, I've lost so, so many dear friends to AIDS related illnesses. I volunteered with BCAP and other organizations and also lost many there. There are a lot of weird sociological quirks as well. For instance, as a very promiscuous twenty-something, I rarely practiced safer sex. It took being a sex worker to actually start using condoms consistently. TBH, medicine has advanced so much that people live regularly to ripe old ages living with HIV like many other auto-immune disorders. Like COVID, there are several strains of HIV. (So, COVID 19 is identified by strain like Hepatitis-B or C or Herpes Simplex 1 or 2, or HIV 1 or 2,...) I see commercials on TV for drugs that help patients achieve U=U (Undetectable=Untransmitible) in which HIV positive patients' viral load is so low they literally test as negative and can't pass the virus on through sex. Yet most of the general public has no knowledge of this or that there are drugs available to prevent catching the virus. People will wear masks to prevent COVID spread but most doctors refuse to prescribe PReP. My partner is HIV+/U=U and I'm on Truvada so I'm not worried about contracting the virus at all. That being said, being an 80s child, fear has been baked into me. Having sat at way too many hospital bedsides as a teen and young person, I admit I have nightmares of my partner there, on a respirator dying as my husband just died. It's terrifying. Right now, with the medical knowledge we have, there is no damn reason at all there isn't a cure. No fucking reason at all. Sorry, you can see I feel passionately about this.

DAVID
50
HE/HIM

I am HIV+. Undetectable and healthy in that aspect. It was a very rough road in the beginning. I was extremely ill. They thought I had leukemia. I also had a lot of different side effects from medications. I finally adjusted to the meds and I've been okay since. Although I have to say that I have never really felt the same since my diagnosis.

MICHAEL
50
HE/HIM/HIS

I have been living with HIV for 18 years. At one point, my TCells and viral load were low enough to declare I had AIDS. I am thankful for the scientific breakthroughs that have allowed living with HIV an option now where it was not for so many before me. Now that I am undetectable and non transmittable, my life has new meaning and purpose. The stigma that I am "dirty" or "tainted," that feeling that I will never be accepted by another lover or soulmate, has gone away and I am forever grateful.

KIMMY
47
HIM/HER

It scared me to death because when the disease reached central New York and I saw the celebrity deaths on the cover of tabloids every week, I chickened out of many opportunities and steered myself toward the hetero lifestyle. Nowadays, there is still fear but moreso, I have feelings of sadness. Sadness for those who lived their lives and paid the price of that nasty disease and also the sadness I carry that I missed out on a lot of life.

JONATHAN
44
HE/HIM

AIDS/HIV has impacted me personally. I had a gay uncle who contracted AIDS back in 1985 at the very beginning of the epidemic. At that time, no one could guess the worldwide impact of the virus. I myself didn't know how my uncle died for a good decade and a half after he passed away. My uncle was vibrant, talented and a great person that was taken too soon. Man, I could have used his advice as I was coming out and I know he would've made a great mentor. A story that stands out to me is when, years later, my aunt told me the story of how she could find no funeral home that would take my uncle. She finally had to call the Los Angeles Gay and Lesbian Center for help. You see this and hear about instances of this happening on TV, but it's an entirely different experience when you have family members that actually lived it.

JV
43
HE/HIM/HIS

Not until recently, we found out my other half was positive. I'm still negative. It's been a journey but now he is undetectable. It's amazing how far medicine has come and how HIV/Aids is controllable.

KAYTI
LOOK 32, FEEL 78, LEGALLY 42
RECENTLY FEMALE (SHE/HER/HERS) TO EVERYONE BUT BLOOD FAMILY

A few close friends have it.

RYAN
39
HE/HIM

For me, it has always been something that has promoted a great deal of self care, and a dedication to staying on top of any and all routine screenings that are suggested.

STEPHEN
38
HE/HIM

It hasn't impacted me personally, other than meeting and becoming dear friends with people who are positive and hearing their stories and their daily lives and unique impacts.

ANDREW
30
PANSEXUAL TRANSGUY—HE/HIM

AIDS/HIV hasn't impacted me directly a ton per say. My sex education, as a student (in the 90s and early 2000s) did see a negative connotation, connection between being a part of the LGBT community, and AIDS/HIV; similarly as it was presented, particularly at the time. In high school and the beginning of college, I would donate blood and plasma. After I came out as a pansexual transguy, someone having relationships with other men, the ban on gay men donating impacted me more directly.

JACKSON
30
HE/HIM/HIS

I have several close friends who are positive. It has the lows of any disease that can be fatal or not.

MISS JESSICA
27
NON-BINARY, ALL PRONOUNS

Me personally, I have only had scares with partners. Otherwise, I have had no direct impact from AIDS/HIV.

PARRISH
23
HE/HIM

MADI
21
SHE/HER

Because of my age and the time I grew up in, AIDS has not had a major impact on me personally, but I cannot understate the profound impact it has had on our community as a whole.

FREYA
20
SHE/HER/HERS

HIV/AIDS has not affected me.

***

The answers in this chapter are particularly telling of the different ages. I'm so glad for scientific advancements that have made HIV/AIDS no longer a death sentence, but I remember when it was. Unfortunately hetero people, before internet and with only the nightly news to get information, did not hear about AIDS/HIV until it affected people who received blood transfusions. It was then blamed on the gay community, who were banned from giving blood and still are to this day. This needs to change.

CHAPTER 12

UNDERGROUND NEWSPAPERS USED TO BE THE WAY PEOPLE GOT NEWS ABOUT THE LGBTQ+ COMMUNITY. HOW HAS THE INTERNET CHANGED OR HELPED THE COMMUNITY?

CORKY
76
MR.

There are various internet sites where GLBTQ+ can get updates about what is happening and interact with others. My favorite is "GLBTQ Nation."

DAVID
69
HE

Underground newspapers weren't always easy to find, especially outside college towns. I think the internet has been a help to the community. I hope no one feels as isolated as I did as a kid. I'm sure there are people who feel isolated and alone, and I hope they can find out that they're not "the only one" sooner than I did. I'm sure the internet has helped.

JW
66

I would say more exposure has probably helped, but I'm not a radical.

ROB
66

I sure wish there had been an internet when I was 13. I knew absolutely nothing. I knew very little about ANY kind of sex.

CJEAN
63
HE/HIM

Bluntly, I think social media had degraded the minds of our society—the anonymous cruelty is a rot impacting everyone—the "influencer" culture is shallow and produces nothing of worth and a sense of entitlement for those who contribute nothing to society. I think availability of information has made it massively easier for young people to find their truth though, if they can wade through the trash. I used to pick up the "fag rags" every week in the bars and loved them.

SHANNON
58

When I was closeted, I used to read magazines all of the time—The Advocate etc. Now I read occasional articles posted by friends, but usually just read mainstream media for news about rights and court cases.

TOM
58

The internet has made so much information available to so many.

TONY
58
HE/HIM

It is probably a godsend that kids struggling with coming out any-where have access to resources that I certainly didn't have during my formative and coming out years. I guess the real issue surrounds the haters and cyberbullies that can make life hell.

CHRISTOPHER
57

The internet has been a game changer, both good and bad. It has made finding helpful resources, even dates, hugely easier. It has made finding "community" to not feel alone far easier. The downside is that it has made cyberbullying and harassment easier also.

GUS
57
HE/HIM

Many are lamenting the "old fashioned way" that gay people could connect (underground papers, gay bars, etc.), but I think that the internet has liberated us. It has made the world smaller, has allowed "kids" to see that there are so many people just like them. Now, we don't need to live underground or in ghettos anymore.

BRAD
54

You used to meet other gay people at bars or church. LOL! Now, you just log on to social media and find them and get the current scoop in the community. I think the close-knit part of the community has changed, as gay bars are closing now due to them not being a "safe haven" for gays. Better that we're more accepted, though.

ANTHONY
53
HE/HIM/HIS

The internet makes it a lot easier to hide behind a computer keyboard and be vile and nasty with your comments. Don't think the newspapers have much relevance today.

JOHN
52
GAY MALE AND HE/HIM/HIS

When used correctly, for the spreading of legit information, the internet and social media can be tremendous sources of information and ways to spread awareness.

MIKE
51
HE/HIM/HIS

It's made it easier to connect with the community.

PASHA
51
SHE/HER OR THEY/THEM

The internet is a double-edged sword. I'm not telling you anything you don't already know. It's been a profound change in the world-wide community for so many marginalized groups. But it's also creating echo chambers for all facets of society via algorithms and personal choices and everyone can get misinformation if we aren't vigilant about fact checking our own social media feeds. We've been able to create new families which is invaluable, but it also encourages larger divides.

DAVID
50
HE/HIM

I feel it's easier to meet other gay people or groups. Also for seeking help and advice.

MICHAEL
50
HE/HIM/HIS

Obviously, curiosity can be satisfied in an instant with the internet; which has its pros and cons. Curious and questioning individuals have an outlet to learn and meet others like them. It can allow us to feel closer to one another through common interests. I feel the bad side of the internet is the fact that it is an opportunity for shallow gratification, not allowing us to interact on a level, less shallow playing field. We no longer have to go out and interact face to face and discover one another in person.

KIMMY
47
HIM/HER

Validation and visibility. I'm not alone in how I feel. We all can't be mentally ill or depraved. We are everywhere. I was unaware of a transgender community and before internet I thought it was straight/bi or gay only. I was unaware of other groups and their subgroups till AOL was available.

JONATHAN
44
HE/HIM

I wish the LGBTQ+ community still got their news from underground newspapers. I would rather get my news and information from newspapers than from most internet sites. I feel that the internet has changed the LGBTQ+ community the same way it has changed the hetero community. It can connect people with resources and support groups they may not know about or have access to.

JV
43
HE/HIM/HIS

So much is out there now, and I feel it helps so many to cope with how to come out and find your community and help with everything.

KAYTI
LOOK 32, FEEL 78, LEGALLY 42
RECENTLY FEMALE (SHE/HER/HERS) TO EVERYONE BUT BLOOD FAMILY

For over 20 years, the internet has allowed chat rooms, news, and information (both valid and not).

Underground newspapers used to be the way people got news about the LGBTQ+ community. How has the internet changed or helped the community?

RYAN
39
HE/HIM

I think that although the internet has made it easy to connect with people, it has also removed a sense of community from Denver. I know I sound old when I say, "Back in my day..." but I do miss gathering and meeting people in person as opposed to relying on apps and the internet to meet.

STEPHEN
38
HE/HIM

ANDREW
30
PANSEXUAL TRANSGUY—HE/HIM

I would say it changed and helped the community for good for the most part. I say this because the internet allows for information about the community to be more easily accessed by any and all.

Also, it allows for people to connect to other members of the community, regardless of an individual's location in the world at any given moment.

JACKSON
30
HE/HIM/HIS

We now can connect with individuals internationally. It has expanded our reach to others and has helped us create a stronger sense of community through social media platforms.

MISS JESSICA
27
NON-BINARY, ALL PRONOUNS

There is information literally EVERYWHERE on ANY topic now! There is no reason kids, parents, and/or queer people in general cannot be educated on anything.

PARRISH
23
HE/HIM

MADI
21
SHE/HER

I think that the internet has been a HUGE help to LGBTQ+ people everywhere. It allows us to find community with others even if we are across the world from each other. There are tons of LGBTQ+ people that are in a place where they can't be themselves in real life for a variety of reasons, but outlets such as social media allow them to be themselves online which is incredibly important. It also allows for a great amount of education to be had by questioning individuals, and is a great resource for people to ask questions or seek advice on how to come out, gender identity, etc.

FREYA
20
SHE/HER/HERS

Social media has grown so much and been so supportive and loving toward this community. More and more people are becoming educated on the entire meaning of LGBTQ+. As well as becoming educated on specific aspects of the community which is so important.

***

A friend and I have plans to track down some of these old underground papers and I can't wait to read them. As for now, truthful information is out there, as is support, and I think that is fantastic. Unfortunately, it comes with downsides of bullying and misinformation. Choose where you get your information carefully. There are LGBTQ+ community centers in every state that will have a list of links to information on their websites.

CHAPTER 13

IF YOU COULD SAY ONE THING TO YOUR YOUNGER SELF... AND WHAT AGE?

CORKY
76
MR.

Given the time and climate of the general public's attitude toward "gays," I wouldn't have changed anything. I "played the game" pretty well. LOL.

DAVID
69
HE

"Just keep it together gurrl."

JW
66

Just be myself 14 years of age and there is nothing wrong with my feelings.

ROB
66

Nah. I did okay.

CJEAN
63
HE/HIM

Don't be afraid to put yourself out there. At 18, when I considered my coming out.

SHANNON
58

I wish I had come out sooner and lived my life instead of being in the closet so many years.

TOM
58

Come out earlier. I wasted and lost so many years.

TONY
58
HE/HIM

You are who you are. Love it, own it, be you. (In my teens.)

CHRISTOPHER
57

I would tell my 16-year-old self to persevere with courage. The road ahead will be daunting, but worth every step. Ignore the haters, they are wrong. About everything. Their hate is simply misplaced anger. The best way to best them is not to. Simply walk away. You have nothing to prove to anybody, except yourself.

GUS
57
HE/HIM

Gus (at 11). You are going to live the best life ever! It will be hard at times, even devastating, but you'll endure. You'll be the father that you always wanted to be and will find the man of your dreams with whom you'll live out the best years of your life.

BRAD
54

"Chill—you're going to survive this."—age 22.

ANTHONY
53
HE/HIM/HIS

Watch your drinking, probably at the age of 16.

JOHN
52
GAY MALE AND HE/HIM/HIS

Be yourself and don't be afraid. Do not let your imagining of how people might think drive your decisions of what is right for you or who you are. Your body and your heart know you better than anyone, listen to them. Age 13—15, I think.

MIKE
51
HE/HIM/HIS

You're going to be okay...at many points in my youth.

PASHA
51
SHE/HER OR THEY/THEM

To my childhood self at every age I can ever remember: It's not your fault! At 15, "Acknowledge your gf publicly and tell everyone else to fuck off!"

DAVID
50
HE/HIM

Be proud of yourself. Maybe 13?

MICHAEL
50
HE/HIM/HIS

Continue to be a creative, outgoing, non apologetic man. Your mom taught you well. When you feel alone, get out of your head as there are so many others like you out there. You're going to do amazing things!

KIMMY
47
HIM/HER

I would tell myself to invest in Microsoft at the age of 16. I would say, get as far away from Central New York and head west asap.

JONATHAN
44
HE/HIM

I would say to my 24-year-old self, "Everything you are going to go through and experience in the next twenty years, good and bad, will lead you to an amazing and loving husband and an amazing and supportive family, both born into and chosen. So keep on truckin'!"

JV
43
HE/HIM/HIS

It truly gets better and easier. Be who you want to be. 15 years old.

KAYTI
LOOK 32, FEEL 78, LEGALLY 42
RECENTLY FEMALE (SHE/HER/HERS) TO EVERYONE BUT BLOOD FAMILY

I wish I could have done something at age 18, but at 23–24, I should have transitioned.

RYAN
39
HE/HIM

Be proud of who you are...love yourself.

STEPHEN
38
HE/HIM

Ask the hard questions of those around you, and don't settle for answers that don't add up just because you feel you need to believe a certain thing to fit in and be accepted. But, to my younger self, I would also say I totally understand why, at that time in your life, you felt you needed to be accepted and fit in, and there's no shame.

ANDREW
30
PANSEXUAL TRANSGUY—HE/HIM

I had a high school vice principal tell me my senior year of high school as graduation approached, "Believe in yourself for you are the only one who will be around for the long run. Be healthy. Be happy. Be good." It was very fitting to me at the time and to this day actually. That is one I would definitely tell myself as early as middle school, even late elementary school age.

JACKSON
30
HE/HIM/HIS

Love yourself, you are beautiful inside and out and you deserve love.

MISS JESSICA
27
NON-BINARY, ALL PRONOUNS

If I were in a safe and loving space, it would be to stop losing time worrying about other people's opinions of yourself. Stop being scared. You only die once, you live every single day. Live for you!

PARRISH
23
HE/HIM

You will be loved for who you are. And I would say it to the little fourth grader. He had it very rough and that's when he started to bury his feelings.

MADI
21
SHE/HER

I would definitely tell little 5th grade Madi that being gay is okay. I know you just learned what this means for you, and that it is scary, and that you have a long tough road ahead of you, but you can do it and life will be so much better when you get to be the real you. You might be different from everyone around you, you might hear jokes about how you feel, and you might not see a lot of characters on TV or in movies that are like you, but that is okay.

FREYA
20
SHE/HER/HERS

I would tell myself to stop chasing after those who don't want you and to love yourself more. I have always struggled with not being myself and following others' actions to fit in. I would want my younger self to know that there are always people who will support you. Even though it might be tough to see them or find them, they will always be there. You will find them eventually.

***

Everyone wants validation earlier in life. What would you say to your younger self?

CHAPTER 14

WHAT IS SOMETHING NOT DIFFERENT FROM STRAIGHT SOCIETY?

CORKY
76
MR.

Love of family and others in our community! Our "straight counterparts" are finally realizing and embracing that "we" are just the same as them; only who we fall in love with is different.

DAVID
69
HE

There's not much that's different at the most basic level. My college rhetoric teacher told me, "Gays do tend to dress better." I've always thought gays were more fun and less apt to be bigots.

JW
66

Not quite sure what this means or how to answer it.

ROB
66

Not sure.

CJEAN
63
HE/HIM

Any human characteristic not related to a same sex attraction. We really are all the same when you get down to the basics. We live, hope, love, thrive, cry, bleed and fail like everyone does.

SHANNON
58

My family life is very similar to straight families. There are a few issues with in-laws, but our day to day is very much like anyone else who has kids and work two jobs.

TOM
58

I'm afraid I don't understand this question.

TONY
58
HE/HIM

I don't think I understand the question and don't want to misunderstand as I might jump on a soapbox unnecessarily. My life in "society" is lived as everyone else. I go shopping, and to the gym, and have a dog, a husband, a nice house and a good job as an attorney. I don't regard any of that as "straight" society, that's just the world we live in.

CHRISTOPHER
57

Similarities with straight society? That's easy. People are people. We all dream, succeed, fail, seek connection. We are all prone to human fallibility. Everyone seems to dwell on the small things that make us different, instead of the 98% of the ways we are the same.

GUS
57
HE/HIM

We all live the same lives, with the same challenges and the same moments of pure joy.

BRAD
54

Gay marriage and partnership. We all go through the same type of issues, problems, day-to-day activities, joys, sorrows. We're not any different. Love is love.

ANTHONY
53
HE/HIM/HIS

We all have the same concerns...crime, taxes, a pandemic.

JOHN
52
GAY MALE AND HE/HIM/HIS

MIKE
51
HE/HIM/HIS

Love.

PASHA
51
SHE/HER OR THEY/THEM

So, so sadly, there are cliques and competition and hate everywhere.

DAVID
50
HE/HIM

That it takes all different kinds of people. And love has no boundaries.

MICHAEL
50
HE/HIM/HIS

Men can be shallow jerks...seriously. Men are usually less sensitive. I don't know if that is part of our DNA or the way we are trained by society. Know that we all love the same, share in common problems and enjoy similar interests.

KIMMY
47
HIM/HER

What I have observed in the last two years is that most of you all hate each other. The backbiting, gossip and general disdain of other queer people was a little shocking. In one instant, everyone is all lov-ey-dovey and preaches community and then they talk shit. I have noticed this not just at the Sunday brunches, but even in the volunteer groups we both participate in.

JONATHAN
44
HE/HIM

N/A

JV
43
HE/HIM/HIS

KAYTI
LOOK 32, FEEL 78, LEGALLY 42
*RECENTLY FEMALE (SHE/HER/HERS) TO EVERYONE BUT
BLOOD FAMILY*

Unsure of the question.

RYAN
39
HE/HIM

I think that we are all looking for the same types of things: companionship, love, happiness. Those things are basic human wants/needs that we all share.

STEPHEN
38
HE/HIM

ANDREW
30
PANSEXUAL TRANSGUY—HE/HIM

Just like any other group of people out there in the world, there are people in the LGBT community that are less then kind, to be nice about it. We are a multifaceted group of people, just like everyone else. We don't fit nicely in a box as a group or as individuals. We, too, have stereotypes and expectations within the community which are not necessarily bad or good, just exist.

JACKSON
30
HE/HIM/HIS

MISS JESSICA
27
NON-BINARY, ALL PRONOUNS

Dating is hard and people are terribly self-centered.

PARRISH
23
HE/HIM

MADI
21
SHE/HER

I think the majority of straight people don't realize that a gay relationship is no different than a straight relationship. We love the same, we feel the same feelings, we eat the same food, we do the same activities. I wish that people would realize this and not ostracize gay relationships as something totally different than straight relationships, because there really is no difference in the most basic of senses.

FREYA
20
SHE/HER/HERS

Something not different from straight society is the fact that we all have a romantic attachment and love for our significant others. Just because we love different people or genders does not mean that our love is any different. I think sometimes just because someone is a part of the LGBTQ+ community, straight people think their love is different. All love is love. I think that is something incredibly important to remember.

***

Go figure, not much difference.

CHAPTER 15

WHAT STEREOTYPE DO YOU FIND MOST AMUSING/ PISSES YOU OFF?

CORKY
76
MR.

The only stereotype that, for so long, was associated with gay men was the portrayal of all being "swishy queens" with such pronounced "feminine gestures & mannerisms." Now that we are accepted in society, people are finding out that there are just as many "manly" and muscular men who definitely don't fit that outdated depiction of who we are.

DAVID
69
HE

I've watched as many of the old stereotypes have faded away. Not all gay men are portrayed as limp-wristed and lisping. One of my favorite stereotypes comes from a friend's mother many years ago. She and my friend were people watching and my friend spotted a nice-looking guy. He asked his mother if she thought he might be gay. She gasped and said that he couldn't be—"Just look at his shoes!"

JW
66

Most amusing—drag queens. Pisses me off—the real feminine type males and butch girls.

ROB
66

I'm fine with it all—if we're the ones poking fun at ourselves.

CJEAN
63
HE/HIM

Amusing: Men on Film—from *In Living Color*

Least: Anything that is demeaning. For years in movies, the gay character had to die at the end or be the brunt of the joke (see *Celluloid Closet*).

SHANNON
58

I think it's hilarious when people ask, "Who is the man?" in the relationship. It's ridiculous! We are equal partners.

I don't like it when people think my relationship isn't equal to heterosexual marriages. I have a colleague that calls my wife my significant other. He asked me one day where we got our kids. I told him they came from Jenny's womb.

TOM
58

Nathan Lane in *The Bird Cage* always makes me laugh. I'm not sure which stereotype pisses me off.

TONY
58
HE/HIM

Stereotypes themselves piss me off. Can we just not?

CHRISTOPHER
57

Stereotype that most pisses me off? That being gay is somehow a "flaw." That we are "deviant" or "predatory."

GUS
57
HE/HIM

Amusing: "the queen" gay man. Pisses me off: equating gay men as pedophiles.

BRAD
54

Gay men are prissy. I love sports, cars, power tools, etc. just as much as any straight guy. Give me a '71 Chevy with a 440 big block engine and I'm in heaven! LOL!

ANTHONY
53
HE/HIM/HIS

They either show someone in very little clothes wearing leather or a drag queen. The LGBTQ community is so much richer than those two stereotypes.

JOHN
52
GAY MALE AND HE/HIM/HIS

(Amusing) That no gays like sports or are athletic or that we are all born decorators or fashionistas. (Pisses me off) That gays are pedophilic, predatory or that we can choose a sexuality. The ignorance over choice versus genetics (nature versus nurture if you will) is probably the most infuriating. I mean if we had the power to convert, then we'd have even more fabulous ranks than we already do! Ha ha!

MIKE
51
HE/HIM/HIS

Nothing in particular comes to mind. Stereotypes exist for a reason, but never apply to everyone in any group.

PASHA
51
SHE/HER OR THEY/THEM

That queer/bi people are promiscuous, faking to land men, or "going through a phase," according to both monosexual gays/lesbians and straights. It's super judgy and weirdly misogynistic.

DAVID
50
HE/HIM

That all gay men are flaming queens.

MICHAEL
50
HE/HIM/HIS

It upsets me when straight people feel that because I am gay, I am more flamboyant and less of what society paints as a "man." All people are different and generally do not fit into just one box.

KIMMY
47
HIM/HER

Amusing—I suppose that we all watch *Queer Eye* or *RuPaul*. I cross-dress frequently and go full drag at the clubs but oddly enough, I've never watched an episode of *RuPaul*. Ever. Pisses me off—I am not going to be your curiosity in the bedroom. And that some people expect you to act a certain way, "But you don't act gay."

JONATHAN
44
HE/HIM

N/A

JV
43
HE/HIM/HIS

That we are all bottoms hah, that we're all effeminate, or we want to have sex with every guy we meet.

KAYTI
LOOK 32, FEEL 78, LEGALLY 42
RECENTLY FEMALE (SHE/HER/HERS) TO EVERYONE BUT BLOOD FAMILY

I am outraged about the standardized media casting of transgender people as sex workers. It only helps to reinforce stereotypes.

RYAN
39
HE/HIM

Gay men are flakey. Not all of us are!

STEPHEN
38
HE/HIM

ANDREW
30
PANSEXUAL TRANSGUY—HE/HIM

The one that comes to mind—the fact that there is still a "man" and "woman" in a non-heterosexual, non-cisgender relationship. This is a very heterosexual, cisgender idea.

JACKSON
30
HE/HIM/HIS

I find it amusing that all gay girls are studs or masculine and all gay boys are extra feminine.

MISS JESSICA
27
NON-BINARY, ALL PRONOUNS

Most amusing—that you can look at someone and figure out how they sexually identify. Pisses me off—that every queer man has AIDS.

PARRISH
23
HE/HIM

If something happens, someone says, "It's because you're gay." It's just such a weird trap to fall into. I do say it sometimes too when I don't feel like handling a situation. When in all reality, it's just a lame thing to say and sometimes a negative connotation.

MADI
21
SHE/HER

There is this weird perpetuating concept floating around mostly religious outlets that gay people are all pedophiles. I can't even begin to describe how wrong this is. Yes, unfortunately, I am sure that there are some LGBTQ+ people that are pedophiles, but the same goes for straight people. I don't think I even know where this idea stems from, but there are a lot of people that think this is true. I also can't stand the stereotype that all gay people are attracted to every single person around them that is the same gender as them. Just because I am friends with a girl doesn't mean that I am attracted to her.

FREYA
20
SHE/HER/HERS

The stereotype that always pisses me off in gay women relationships is when people ask which one is the "guy" in the relationship? People always think one of us has to be more masculine or butch. In reality, both can be more feminine or masculine. It just depends on the relationship. I get asked that question too often.

***

Stereotypes of any kind are bad and don't encompass most people in a group or community. The LGBTQ+ community seems to have been overly stereotyped and only more visibility will get rid of that.

CHAPTER 16

WHAT DO YOU FEEL IS THE BIGGEST MISCONCEPTION ABOUT THE LGBTQ+ COMMUNITY?

CORKY
76
MR.

I feel the biggest misconception is with straight men thinking that if they go to a gay bar with women friends or even gay friends, they will have to "endure" gay guys coming on to them constantly. LOL. True, the better looking they are, the more they will be noticed, yet the club is full of equally handsome hunks, so no need to flatter themselves too much! When approached, which they will be, a simple "hey thanks, but I'm straight" will suffice for the guy to look elsewhere. ;-)

DAVID
69
HE

Just how many of us are out there and that there are many gay "communities." It's not a homogenous group anymore than heterosexuals are.

I once had a co-worker nearly drive off the road when I told him I smoked pot. His response was "but you're so straight." I laughed and told him that not only did I smoke pot, but I was gay. That's when we nearly hit the guardrail. (We became good friends and he called me several years ago just to be sure I had lived through the plague.)

JW
66

That we are all just interested in sex.

ROB
66

Pedophilia! That drives me insane. And that we have an "agenda," as if equal rights for everybody is somehow bad.

CJEAN
63
HE/HIM

Homogenous in some way—there is one gay thing—every straight woman needs a BFF to go shop with—portraying us as two dimensional.

SHANNON
58

I think the biggest misconception that people have about our community is that we choose to be gay. Though I am very happy with who I am, it is not something I would choose. It has been a very difficult journey and it would have been much easier to be straight, especially with my family and faith background.

TOM
58

I think the biggest misconception about our community is that we want special rights over everybody else's, which of course isn't the case.

TONY
58
HE/HIM

That we are all alike and that we know everyone else who is gay. "Oh, I have a gay friend in [fill in the blank], do you know them?" Or that one gay or lesbian person can speak for the entire community, as if we all think, act, and believe the same. It is really ignorant.

CHRISTOPHER
57

I think that the biggest misconception about the LGBTQ community is that we are shallow and physically obsessed. Some of the most gifted people I have ever known were gay.

GUS
57
HE/HIM

The biggest misconception is that we are all sex starved, living a life of vice and depravity.

BRAD
54

That we're a threat to the straight way of life and marriage. We just want to live our life every day just like straight people want to live their life—in peace.

ANTHONY
53
HE/HIM/HIS

Hard to answer.

JOHN
52
GAY MALE AND HE/HIM/HIS

That we have an agenda that includes making more people gay. Our agenda, IMO, is to be treated like human beings in every aspect. But, that is the case for all persons of any (often multiple at the same time) minority.

MIKE
51
HE/HIM/HIS

That we're somehow deviant.

PASHA
51
SHE/HER OR THEY/THEM

That we're all child molesters.

DAVID
50
HE/HIM

That we want special treatment. When all that we really want is equality.

MICHAEL
50
HE/HIM/HIS

That we are less than, cast into the shadows where we belong to do things that "heathens" do.

KIMMY
47
HIM/HER

That we are Godless, depraved sex addicts or pedophiles. That we want to convert others.

JONATHAN
44
HE/HIM

I feel the biggest misconception about the LGBTQ+ is that we are a monolith. That we all love each other in a big "buy the world a Coke" kind of situation. It's just not true. There is a lot of hate and judgement out there. Just take a gander at FB.

JV
43
HE/HIM/HIS

That we don't care for our own. It's really sad that there is still so much hate in our community. Whether it comes from the older crowd that came before us, but I feel that today's generation has it pretty easy and we need to be more careful with how we carry ourselves and be there for each other.

KAYTI
LOOK 32, FEEL 78, LEGALLY 42
RECENTLY FEMALE (SHE/HER/HERS) TO EVERYONE BUT BLOOD FAMILY

They are valid tax paying people that deserve equal rights. Many people don't feel that way.

RYAN
39
HE/HIM

I think that people see the gay party scene, and they assume that all LGBTQ+ individuals are wild and reckless. There are many of us who are movers and shakers, and who excel and succeed in our careers and in life.

STEPHEN
38
HE/HIM

ANDREW
30
PANSEXUAL TRANSGUY—HE/HIM

Either that we are just our LGBTQ+ identity or that we have an agenda (usually a bad one it seems).

JACKSON
30
HE/HIM/HIS

MISS JESSICA
27
NON-BINARY, ALL PRONOUNS

That we choose to be queer. Which in a weird way we do, but not for the reasons people like to think.

PARRISH
23
HE/HIM

MADI
21
SHE/HER

I think that the biggest misconception about our community is that we are all softies, or we are all emotionally insecure. This is just flat out not true. The people I know and look up to in the LGBTQ+ community are some of the strongest people I know, because we spend our entire lives just trying to exist without the ridicule of straight people, and constantly having to "prove" ourselves and defend ourselves. Coming out is so extremely hard, I can't even put into words what it feels like. Simply the act of coming out takes a great deal of strength, and requires a level of emotional strength and maturity and determination that I think a great deal of people dismiss, or don't realize.

FREYA
20
SHE/HER/HERS

I think everyone has this idea that every gay person is very flamboyant and likes to "flaunt" their sexuality. In reality, love is love and people are people. Some people may act more outwardly flamboyant or excited compared to others. Just because you've met one person who is like that, does not mean every person is going to be like that.

***

As with anything, no matter why you are reading this book, check your preconceived notions at the door.

CHAPTER 17

WHO DO YOU THINK IS THE BEST PUBLIC FIGURE FOR THE LGBT COMMUNITY? / THE WORST?

CORKY
76
MR.

Both Governor Jared Polis and Colorado's First Gentleman, Marlon Reis, are exceptional "out" public figures! Also, who would have thought that a "gay man" could run for President and get "primary votes"! Hooray for Mayor Pete Buttigieg! The absolute worst are the "conservative Christian clergy" who continue to preach the "evils of homosexuality"!

DAVID
69
HE

I've got to go with Mayor Pete on this one. For the worst, point at any number of Republicans, many of whom I suspect are closet cases.

JW
66

Best public figure, Mayor Pete and Anderson Cooper. Worst public figure, Caitlyn Jenner and Paula Poundstone.

ROB
66

I think that news professionals such as Rachel Maddow, Anderson Cooper and Don Lemon are an inspiration. Also gay congress people.

CJEAN
63
HE/HIM

Best: Pete Buttigieg
Worst: Milo Yiannopoulos

SHANNON
58

For my generation, Ellen was the best public figure for the community. She was the first person to normalize being gay.

TOM
58

I think the best public figures for our community are Mayor Pete and Jared Polis. I think the worst public figure for our community is Caitlyn Jenner, by light years.

TONY
58
HE/HIM
Well, Pete Buttigieg ranks up there among the best. Ellen DeGeneres ranks pretty high, too, especially for her courage many years ago. The worst? Lindsey Graham, that despicable closet case, is worse than the worst.

CHRISTOPHER
57
Best and worst public figures? Billy Porter and Milo Yiannopoulos.

GUS
57
HE/HIM
The best public figure is Pete Buttigieg, because he's the first to "normalize" that a gay person could be President of the United States. The worst: Milo Yiannopoulos because he's a cretin.

BRAD
54
Rachel Maddow is one of the best, in my opinion. She is smart, articulate, in a wonderful relationship, and doesn't seem to get caught up in controversy. David Bromstad is one that I have a hard time with, but I think we're just on different pages.

ANTHONY
53
HE/HIM/HIS
There are so many, it would be difficult to name one as there is not just one. Same comment for the worst.

JOHN
52
GAY MALE AND HE/HIM/HIS

MIKE
51
HE/HIM/HIS

No thoughts on that.

PASHA
51
SHE/HER OR THEY/THEM

Of course, Harvey Milk, but Bayard Rustin isn't nearly well known enough as well as Marsha P Johnson, Christine Jorgensen, James Baldwin, Oscar Wilde, Alice Dunbar Nelson, David Bowie, Sylvia Rivera and Barbara Gittings. There are seemingly fewer LGBTQIA role models that suck but Milo Yiannopoulos, Joe Dallas, Kevin Spacey, Bryan Singer and Donnie McClurkin come to mind.

DAVID
50
HE/HIM

Got to love RuPaul! I cannot stand Caitlyn Jenner!

MICHAEL
50
HE/HIM/HIS

KIMMY
47
HIM/HER

Best = Lady Gaga. Worst = I don't know—I suppose any anti lgbt evangelical or politician who gets outed in scandal.

JONATHAN
44
HE/HIM

I gotta say, that right now, the best public figure for the LGBTQ+ community is the new Secretary of Transportation, Pete Buttigieg. I mean, the heights we can aspire to, as an individual or a community. The worst? Ellen, Lance Bass and NPH.

JV
43
HE/HIM/HIS

I love Lady Gaga, Pete Buttigieg, and I love Billy Porter also. The Peloton community of instructors are amazing. / The worst? Eh, not any I can think of really.

KAYTI
LOOK 32, FEEL 78, LEGALLY 42
RECENTLY FEMALE (SHE/HER/HERS) TO EVERYONE BUT BLOOD FAMILY

I have spoken about this before, but because certain popular drag queens made a living from embodying #16, I consider them a poor role model.

RYAN
39
HE/HIM

STEPHEN
38
HE/HIM

ANDREW
30
PANSEXUAL TRANSGUY—HE/HIM

I admittedly don't know; I am not the most aware of who's who of the public figures in the LGBT community.

JACKSON
30
HE/HIM/HIS

MISS JESSICA
27
NON-BINARY, ALL PRONOUNS

Best? Lavern Cox. Worst? Caitlyn Jenner.

PARRISH
23
HE/HIM

MADI
21
SHE/HER

I think that Billy Porter is the best public voice for the LGBTQ+ community. He is extremely knowledgeable on the community, and as a BIPOC artist, he encompasses a part of our community that faces extra bigotry and hate. I think that Jeffree Star is an extremely terrible example of the LGBTQ+ community to a large group of people, and unfortunately is extremely famous. He is just a shitty person all around (not to mention extremely racist), and he does not represent the rest of us in the slightest.

FREYA
20
SHE/HER/HERS

The best public figure I would say is our Colorado Governor Polis. As a man in the world of politics, I think it is incredible that he is openly gay with a family. I think Governor Polis has been important in the LGBTQ+ community. A public figure I do not like is Ellen DeGeneres. I don't think she is a very nice person and she is not a good figure to the community.

***

I love that there are political figures listed here because if I had written this book just five years ago this would not have been the case. Clearly more representation is needed but there are some incredible people listed.

CHAPTER 18

WHAT DOES PRIDE MEAN TO YOU?

CORKY
76
MR.

To me, Pride means holding our heads high, knowing that "we" are here for a reason and all of our struggles have been worth it! Again, the more that we are "given a chance," we amaze everyone with our ability to give love and help to those who need it most! I am on the Board of Directors of Feeding Denver's Hungry, a "primarily gay" non-profit organization that provides food to those individuals and families who find not enough money to buy food at the end of the month. Since the COVID pandemic has ravished the entire world, there are so many in our GLBTQ+ community who are devastated with the loss of bars, clubs and restaurants we frequent, therefore putting them "out of work." Starting in March, in addition to our once a month food "hand up," we added another way of helping those struggling in our community. We are blessed in obtaining so many new grants that allow us to provide both of our "food give-aways," more food staples than we ever could have imagined. Every one of us are volunteers, so we, along with others who come out on our "need days" (when we must prepare all the food) can as we call it "go shopping" to take as much food as we want. Months ago, Jim Scharper,our leader who founded this remarkable non-profit, said, "Just in case everything could shut down again, I want all of you to have full pantries." How "farsighted" that was, even more so now, when there are some fanatic people out there who truly want a "civil war" in our country! I did vary from the topic of "Pride," yet it's all in our "Hearts of Gold." :-)

DAVID
69
HE

As someone who feels uncomfortable in crowds, the festivals are of little interest to me. I think the most positive meaning for me is that it helps people in or out of the closet become more comfortable with their feelings, especially the young.

JW
66

Freedom to be me without any discrimination.

ROB
66

I'm not a "crowd" person, but I recognize how important it is to many people.

CJEAN
63
HE/HIM

Freedom—I am not subject to your judgment—my life is not by your definition.

SHANNON
58

Pride has been a movement where LGBTQ can gather and find community. I have been to many pride events and have found them to be affirming.

TOM
58

Equality.

TONY
58
HE/HIM

Celebration, history, the future.

CHRISTOPHER
57

Pride means inclusiveness and celebration of our uniqueness and differences.

GUS
57
HE/HIM

It's a celebration of our ability to live free lives and to love who we choose.

BRAD
54

Being proud of who you are as a person, regardless of what people think of you. I learned a long time ago that you can't make everyone like you, so just stop trying. It's exhausting!

ANTHONY
53
HE/HIM/HIS

Celebration! Freedom!

JOHN
52
GAY MALE AND HE/HIM/HIS

Looking in the mirror and not feeling ashamed.

MIKE
51
HE/HIM/HIS

Being proud of who you are.

PASHA
51
SHE/HER OR THEY/THEM

Not being ashamed.

DAVID
50
HE/HIM

Being proud of yourself whatever you are. Gay, straight, trans and so on.

MICHAEL
50
HE/HIM/HIS

Pride comes from inside, a feeling that through work and struggle, you can stand up with others like you that stand on the shoulders of those that have come before and publicly say, "I am equal, I am strong and I belong."

KIMMY
47
HIM/HER

It means I can celebrate my true self.

JONATHAN
44
HE/HIM

Pride, to me, means just being proud of who you are. Plain and simple. In the words of singer Heather Small, "What have you done today to make you feel proud?"

JV
43
HE/HIM/HIS

Happy, unafraid, no bounds. I am ME and no one can take it away.

KAYTI
LOOK 32, FEEL 78, LEGALLY 42
RECENTLY FEMALE (SHE/HER/HERS) TO EVERYONE BUT BLOOD FAMILY

Living your truth.

RYAN
39
HE/HIM

„Pride" means loving yourself.

STEPHEN
38
HE/HIM

ANDREW
30
PANSEXUAL TRANSGUY—HE/HIM

Pride is both celebrating and fighting for who you are, truly as a member of the LGBTQ community. This sense of pride can also be applied to other aspects of a person's identity—pride in their heritage as another example.

JACKSON
30
HE/HIM/HIS

MISS JESSICA
27
NON-BINARY, ALL PRONOUNS

Pride is unapologetic, authentic self expression.

PARRISH
23
HE/HIM

MADI
21
SHE/HER

Pride means going about life living as your true self without the worry of hate coming from other people, and not caring if it does.

FREYA
20
SHE/HER/HERS

Pride to me means being your truest self. I think it means you are unapologetically proud of who you are.

***

"Pride" is a powerful word! I celebrate every one of you.

CHAPTER 19
IS "GAYDAR" REAL?

CORKY
76
MR.

At one time it really was safe to say that there was "gaydar," but not anymore! With the "common stereotypes" (#16) falling away and the "masculine/feminine appearances" becoming fluid, no one can ever be sure! And, does it really matter anyway? LOL.

DAVID
69
HE

No, I too often confused it with my "please be gaydar."

JW
66

Yes.

ROB
66

Oh hell yes!

Is "gaydar" real?

The Stonewall Uprising? The Marriage Equality Act? Something else?   200

CJEAN
63
HE/HIM

Absolutely. Not 100%, but it was easier years ago—not as easy any-more. Straight boys are so much more relaxed now, so there are many false positives. There used to be a three second rule if they held eye contact, they were gay.

SHANNON
58

Yes! Gaydar is real.

TOM
58

Yes, gaydar is real. I don't have it, but it is real.

TONY
58
HE/HIM

Oh hell yes!

CHRISTOPHER
57

Yes, "gaydar" is real. I have always considered it the "it takes one to know one" phenomenon.

GUS
57
HE/HIM

Yup, mine is accurate 85% of the time.

BRAD
54

Yeah, but being attentive to people's speech and actions is mostly what you call "gaydar." Mine isn't always accurate as I get older. Young people are so open these days!

ANTHONY
53
HE/HIM/HIS

Probably not, but the community likes to think so.

JOHN
52
GAY MALE AND HE/HIM/HIS

For sure! Even people who aren't hiding per se haven't grown into their gay selves yet.

MIKE
51
HE/HIM/HIS

Yes, but not always accurate.

PASHA
51
SHE/HER OR THEY/THEM

Only in the sense that some people are more adept at picking up social cues, body language, etc. that may clue them in to someone's orientation.

Is "gaydar" real?

The Stonewall Uprising? The Marriage Equality Act? Something else?   200

DAVID
50
HE/HIM

Oh yeah! LOL.

MICHAEL
50
HE/HIM/HIS

Yes.

KIMMY
47
HIM/HER

I'm oblivious to it. Since I came out so late in life, I don't know the code, the secret handshake, or the markers that everyone else seems to know. In the cases where I suspected someone was gay, I was way wrong.

JONATHAN
44
HE/HIM

If it is, I don't have it.

JV
43
HE/HIM/HIS

It used to be. Ha! Not so much anymore. LOL!

KAYTI
LOOK 32, FEEL 78, LEGALLY 42
RECENTLY FEMALE (SHE/HER/HERS) TO EVERYONE BUT BLOOD FAMILY

No? Someone is only as clockable as they allow themselves to be. My transgender life is masked unless I want someone to know.

RYAN
39
HE/HIM

It sure is! There is some kind of energetic connection that you can feel from others.

STEPHEN
38
HE/HIM

ANDREW
30
PANSEXUAL TRANSGUY—HE/HIM

Yes and no I would say. Some people do give off "vibes" so to speak that indicate that they are a part of the LGBTQ community, but others are better at hiding them. Also, these "vibes" are not always accurate, and just something along the lines of wishful thinking.

JACKSON
30
HE/HIM/HIS

Is "gaydar" real?

The Stonewall Uprising? The Marriage Equality Act? Something else? 200

MISS JESSICA
27
NON-BINARY, ALL PRONOUNS

Yes, but not always accurate seeing as there are so many ways to identify. But you can tell a lot when people are "in the family."

PARRISH
23
HE/HIM

MADI
21
SHE/HER

Gaydar is 100% a legitimate thing. It is like this underlying connection gay people have with each other, like a nonverbal conversation we have intentionally or unintentionally. I fully stand by the fact that no straight person has gaydar though.

FREYA
20
SHE/HER/HERS

Gaydar is 100% real. Obviously, I think it is solely for those who are gay or a part of the LGBTQ+ community but it is very much real!

***

Well, there you go.

CHAPTER 20

WHAT HAS BEEN YOUR BEST DAY AS AN LGBTQ+ PERSON?

CORKY
76
MR.

There have been far too many "best days," as an openly gay man, these past 15 years for me to ever pick one! From back in (about) 2010, being picked as one of Denver's Hottest Studs (at 66 years old) to being on the cover of *Out Front* in 2012! So many times I've felt, it can't get any better, then it does :-)!

DAVID
69
HE

Probably the first time I walked into a gay bar. I didn't even know such places existed.

JW
66

Being accepted by my nieces.

ROB
66

Every day, even at the lowest.

CJEAN
63
HE/HIM

One day—wow. Best gay day may be when I marched in the first Pride Parade in my home town or my first March on Washington (several days).

SHANNON
58

The best day of my life was the day that I got married to Jenny. We had a church wedding, though it wasn't legal to be married in North Carolina. There were hundreds of people there from both of our churches (I was a music director at a Lutheran church at the time). Our ceremony was beautiful. The weather was perfect. My siblings and Jenny's dad were there, so we had some family support. We had to have two receptions. One at the church with cake and drinks, and then a private reception for a smaller group. There was great food, dancing, love and laughter. (We got married legally a few months later in Washington, D.C.)

TOM
58

My best was the day I married my husband. I probably would not have come out if not for him. He saved me.

TONY
58
HE/HIM

Toss ups. Testifying before City Council and the standing ovation when our ordinance passed. Getting married (legal in D.C. at the time, but not nationwide). The night the Supreme Court issued its decision on gay marriage.

CHRISTOPHER
57

My best day as an LGBTQAI person is each new day. To still be here to share my experiences despite the fire I have walked through to get here.

GUS
57
HE/HIM

Today and every day. I have survived and thrived, have the best man in the world, and two wonderful children with whom I share my life, and a family of choice whom I love. I'm blessed.

BRAD
54

The day marriage equality was enacted! Hands down!

ANTHONY
53
HE/HIM/HIS

Civil Unions in Colorado in 2018. Being the second couple to be recognized.

JOHN
52
GAY MALE AND HE/HIM/HIS

Far too many to recount honestly.

When my dad invited my husband and me to stay in the same room with them was pretty big. Marriage equality was huge! Seeing the White House rainbow lighting scheme was not something I thought I would see in my lifetime. AIDS becoming a lifelong illness versus a death sentence (not a single day but still).

MIKE
51
HE/HIM/HIS

Being in New York for World Pride, in front of the Stonewall Inn, on the 50th anniversary of the Stonewall Riots, waiting for the parade to start and my boyfriend proposing to me in front of hundreds of people. They all went wild when I said yes. It was an amazing moment!

PASHA
51
SHE/HER OR THEY/THEM

The first Parasol Patrol event that brought over 100 volunteers together to shield kids at Mile High Comics from protesters.

DAVID
50
HE/HIM

The day I met my partner! ♥

MICHAEL
50
HE/HIM/HIS

The day I won Mr. International Gay Rodeo Association 1996. It forever changed my life.

KIMMY
47
HIM/HER

I'm still waiting for it.

JONATHAN
44
HE/HIM

June 26th, 2015, when gay marriage was legalized in all 50 states.

JV
43
HE/HIM/HIS

When I got to marry my best friend and husband and it was loud and proud!

KAYTI
LOOK 32, FEEL 78, LEGALLY 42
RECENTLY FEMALE (SHE/HER/HERS) TO EVERYONE BUT BLOOD FAMILY

So far, telling my program director before getting a job offer that I was going to transition and they were acknowledging that.

RYAN
39
HE/HIM

This is probably a horrible answer, but every day is a great day as an LGBTQ+ person. I live my truth every day, and I never feel as if I am not living my authentic life.

STEPHEN
38
HE/HIM

Any day I get to sing on stage with my Denver Gay Men's Chorus, but most especially singing at Carnegie Hall in 2019 for the 50th Anniversary of Stonewall with my parents in the audience having come out on Facebook right before the performance, and then marching in the Global Pride Parade in NYC a couple days later.

ANDREW
30
PANSEXUAL TRANSGUY—HE/HIM

I have a few. One is when my name change became official, legal. When I got my first dose of testosterone. When people around me made the adjustments with my name and pronouns. When I got called sir by someone I didn't know for the first time/didn't question that I'm male. Seeing little events like these actually are impactful on a transperson; it's validating our identities in a positive manor.

JACKSON
30
HE/HIM/HIS

MISS JESSICA
27
NON-BINARY, ALL PRONOUNS

The day I came out to everyone.

PARRISH
23
HE/HIM

I was in NYC in 2017 for an internship and I went to the NYC Pride Parade by myself. And it was the first time I was able to just celebrate, and watch others celebrate the amazing lives we have as members of the LGBTQ+ community. I remember spending all day watching people kiss, cheer, have their kids on their shoulders, and be surrounded by love. I was just me.

MADI
21
SHE/HER

I think that pride fest is always so much fun and so uplifting, but my best day of my LGBTQ+ life was my senior prom. I got to go with my girlfriend, and that was really my big coming out to everyone. We were so excited to go together, and we posted pictures of it on various social media spaces and received an astounding amount of support.

FREYA
20
SHE/HER/HERS

I think my best day is any day that I can go out and be myself with my girlfriend. Any time I get to hold her hand or be around her is my

182

best day. Especially if I can be with her in public and not get dirty looks/nasty stares.

***

So many days to celebrate!

CHAPTER 21

WHO WAS THE FIRST OPENLY GAY CHARACTER YOU SAW IN A MOVIE OR ON TV? WHO WAS THE FIRST ONE YOU SAW THAT YOU FELT ACTUALLY REPRESENTED YOU, OR HAVE YOU YET?

CORKY
76
MR.

The first and (probably) main character who comes to mind, is Ellen! Back in April, 1997, when the general public was beginning to meet and know "gay people," she had two episodes of her popular TV show dedicated to "coming out." This was followed by the cover on *Time* (magazine) with her photo and the words, "Yep, I'm gay." Hooray for her bravery, at that time :-).

DAVID
69
HE

In the last several years there have been great changes in the way gays and lesbians are portrayed on TV and in movies. One of the first gay novels I read was *The Runner*. As I remember, it didn't have a happy ending, but the characters were not stereotypically gay but were people with whom I could relate. So many gay characters on TV and in the movies did not come to a good end. That's changed for the most part. People aren't made to feel like there is something wrong with the characters and that they must be in someway punished.

JW
66

Ellen DeGeneres. I haven't felt that anyone has represented myself.

ROB
66

I think it was *Tales of the City*. It was surreal. They were just like my friends.

CJEAN
63
HE/HIM

TV: He fooled Archie Bunker—Steve, played by Philip Carey, in 1971's *All in the Family*. And Jodie Dallas (Billy Crystal) on *Soap* (1977).
Movie: The cowardly lion and the tin man in *The Wizard of Oz* (1939). *Making Love* (1982) with Michael Ontkean's Zach, who is married to Claire (Kate Jackson) but exploring his homosexuality with Harry Hamlin's Bart.

SHANNON
58
Ellen.

TOM
58

First: Do Paul Lynde and Liberace count? I don't know that I have seen someone who actually represents me, but I really like and admire the TV newsmen, Thomas Roberts and Anderson Cooper.

TONY
58
HE/HIM

First openly gay character: *Dynasty*.
Representational: *And the Band Played On. Angels in America.*

CHRISTOPHER
57

Aidan Quinn in *An Early Frost*. Every one since has represented me to one degree or another.

GUS
57
HE/HIM

Snagglepuss (from Hanna-Barbera fame). *Who was the first one you saw that you felt actually represented you, or have you yet:* Will from *Will and Grace.*

BRAD
54

They weren't gay, but the movie, *Brokeback Mountain,* really hit home for me, especially growing up in a farming/ranching community. The characters seem to tug at my heart the way my feelings did as I was growing up. Actual gay person is difficult, since I feel they aren't really themselves on TV or in the movies as they would be in real life.

ANTHONY
53
HE/HIM/HIS

I don't believe I can name one.

JOHN
52
GAY MALE AND HE/HIM/HIS

MIKE
51
HE/HIM/HIS

No one in particular.

PASHA
51
SHE/HER OR THEY/THEM

Rickie Vasquez in *My So-Called Life*. Maybe Margaret Cho. Being Korean, identifying as queer, we have a lot of parallel life experiences.

DAVID
50
HE/HIM

I guess he wasn't really gay, but I always think of John Ritter in *Three's Company*. Plus I had a crush on him. Lol.

MICHAEL
50
HE/HIM/HIS

KIMMY
47
HIM/HER

JONATHAN
44
HE/HIM

The first openly gay character I remember seeing was "Gabriel" in the 1999 movie, *Trick*. But the character I felt kind of represented me was "Michael" from *Queer As Folk*. Michael was nice, a comic book nerd, and wanted that meaningful relationship. A meaningful relationship is something I always wanted.

JV
43
HE/HIM/HIS

Ellen! *Who was the first one you saw that you felt actually represented you, or have you yet?* Ellen, for sure.

KAYTI
LOOK 32, FEEL 78, LEGALLY 42
RECENTLY FEMALE (SHE/HER/HERS) TO EVERYONE BUT BLOOD FAMILY

Designing Women. Night Court. Who was the first one you saw that you felt actually represented you, or have you yet? Through empathy, I can relate to many, but I haven't seen a sincere media depiction.

Who was the first openly gay character you saw in a movie or on TV?
Who was the first one you saw that you felt actually represented you, or have you yet?

RYAN
39
HE/HIM

The first gay character that I remember seeing was Richard Simmons. The person that most represents me is probably David from *Schitt's Creek*!

STEPHEN
38
HE/HIM

ANDREW
30
PANSEXUAL TRANSGUY—HE/HIM

The first one I remember is Ellen when she came out. Since then, individuals I actually identify with would be Chaz Bono, Laverne Cox and Elliot Page.

JACKSON
30
HE/HIM/HIS

Ellen was my first representation of self before my transition. To this day, I still honor her contributions to our community. She is braver than most!

MISS JESSICA
27
NON-BINARY, ALL PRONOUNS

I am unsure of this one.

PARRISH
23
HE/HIM

MADI
21
SHE/HER

When I got my first phone, I would go on the internet and watch a little show called *The L Word*. It was about a bunch of gay women living their various lives in California. I think it really helped me realize that you can in fact live a normal life as a gay woman, and looking back, the show did a really good job of giving accurate representations of day-to-day life/comments made to gay women. There was one character in particular that I resonated with named Dana. She was a major athlete, and was extremely scared to come out because she was so involved in the world of sports, which is typically not the most accepting space for gay people. I was little miss athlete when I was little, so seeing her deal with this was really important to me.

FREYA
20
SHE/HER/HERS

Probably the shows *Modern Family* or *How to Get Away with Murder* were the first few shows that I saw openly gay television characters. I don't think I've really watched a show where I resonate with a character. I feel as though in a lot of movies and TV shows they play heavily on stereotypes.

Who was the first openly gay character you saw in a movie or on TV? Who was the first one you saw that you felt actually represented you, or have you yet?

***

So there are out characters, but clearly more and authentic representation is needed. We're getting there.

CHAPTER 22

WHAT IS YOUR WORST BULLYING EXPERIENCE?

CORKY
76
MR.

I touched on "bullying" back in #9, but my heart goes out to all the unfortunate young people who, just trying to be themselves, are targets for being singled out and made to feel that they are "less than human." With society being at a point where there is so much anger toward others who are different, children pick up this at home and feel the need to inflict "their meanness" on anyone who can't fight back...usually gay teens! The rate of teen suicide is so much on the rise and even when homosexuality is more accepted than ever, the young kids are still prey for being humiliated, picked on and even physically abused.

DAVID
69
HE

I was bullied when I was a kid, but everyone knew I had several older siblings and never pushed it too far. It was a small town, so everyone knew everyone. I was probably bullied more by one of my older brothers than by anyone else. He was a jock, something I never was. (It wasn't until I was in my 60s that I found out I have a stigma in both eyes and had never been able to accurately see in three dimensions. So, a career as a baseball player was out of the question.) It turned out that we are closer politically than we are with anyone else in the family but we're still not close.

JW
66

Being told by my sister that God doesn't accept my homosexuality.

ROB
66

CJEAN
63
HE/HIM

I am lucky—see #8.

SHANNON
58

I don't really have any bullying experiences. I was closeted for so long. No one knew about me until it was more acceptable.

TOM
58

I have never been bullied for being gay. Other bullying did take place in school.

TONY
58
HE/HIM

I was about 28 waiting in the lobby of my apartment building, when a man approaches and yells "fucking faggot" and proceeds to punch me in the face.

It doesn't really happen any more that someone yells homophobic slurs (I've chosen to live in very progressive places—D.C. and now Oregon), but on the rare occasion someone might yell "faggot," I generally respond with "thank you for noticing." The reaction is priceless.

CHRISTOPHER
57

Worst bullying experience? I'm fortunate in that I really can't recall one.

GUS
57
HE/HIM

I have never had a classic "bullying" experience. I was relentlessly teased as a "heavy" child. My teasing nickname was "T-Tuba." My father would call me Fat Albert. (Hey-hey-hey was his "tease" whenever I decided to eat a sweet snack.)

BRAD
54

Being called "faggot" in middle school and beat up on the playground. Very humiliating and degrading.

194

ANTHONY
53
HE/HIM/HIS

High school. It's why I hated high school. I was never physically bullied, but mentally bullied by some.

JOHN
52
GAY MALE AND HE/HIM/HIS

In 8th grade, a couple friends from school and I had a camp out. It was the onset of puberty for all of us. We talked about the usual stuff; girls, our bodies, playing with ourselves. We all admitted that we did that and we had the awkward circle jerk. One of the three told everyone at school so I became a social outcast. I have always just characterized it as teens being horrible to each other which was (possibly is still) so common place. In hindsight though, I guess you would have to say it was a form of bullying. It certainly hurt me terribly and prolly added to my years of choosing to be closeted. It also pushed me to look beyond those people and grow, and made me more independent. All bad comes with some good, but still it was pretty shitty at the time.

MIKE
51
HE/HIM/HIS

Too many to name one, but I don't think about that shit.

PASHA
51
SHE/HER OR THEY/THEM

After I came forward and testified against the CU Athletics Program in the Football Rape Scandal, I was publicly spat upon and had hot coffee thrown on me by strangers. Others stood by and let it happen without intervening. One particularly humiliating encounter happened in front of my son. Being called a child molester and child sex trafficking groomer and the, "Hillary of Mile High Comics Pizza Gate," through a bull horn kinda sucked. Online QAnon harassment after I livestreamed taking down one of their signs. Literally hundreds of death and rape threats. So many specifically referenced putting me through a wood chipper.

DAVID
50
HE/HIM

Being hit on the head with a hammer handle and was beat up a different time in high school pretty severely.

MICHAEL
50
HE/HIM/HIS

KIMMY
47
HIM/HER

It had nothing to do with lgbt issues. It had everything to do with being poor. I had been bullied and made fun of and called queer and gay but really it wasn't the point they were making. Their point was that I lived in a trailer park.

What is your worst bullying experience?

The Stonewall Uprising? The Marriage Equality Act? Something else?   200

JONATHAN
44
HE/HIM

N/A

JV
43
HE/HIM/HIS

Mostly grade school through early high school. I now know it was jealousy mostly. So many guys were jealous because all the girls wanted to be with me! Haha!

KAYTI
LOOK 32, FEEL 78, LEGALLY 42
RECENTLY FEMALE (SHE/HER/HERS) TO EVERYONE BUT BLOOD FAMILY

Non trans related, I was suspended for being teased. It's possible my harassment was related to my awkwardness because of being trans.

RYAN
39
HE/HIM

I was threatened with a knife in a parking lot when I was in college.

STEPHEN
38
HE/HIM

High school sophomore—senior years—it's all a blur.

ANDREW
30
PANSEXUAL TRANSGUY—HE/HIM

There is not one specific event or incident. But a bunch of times, when someone purposefully and in a malicious manner has chosen to not use my proper pronouns/name. Also, a handful of times of other verbal harassments.

JACKSON
30
HE/HIM/HIS

I guess the worst bully has been President Trump and his administration. They took away protections for transgender healthcare patients and placed bans against transgender soldiers.

MISS JESSICA
27
NON-BINARY, ALL PRONOUNS

Worst is inside my own community from other queer people that thought they were protecting someone when they were destroying them.

PARRISH
23
HE/HIM

MADI
21
SHE/HER

Probably the one I mentioned earlier about my college roommate experience.

FREYA
20
SHE/HER/HERS

My worst bullying experience definitely came from when I was in high school. I was called out a lot for being gay. I knew a girl who was openly very religious and did not like gay people. I had not come out at this point, but she called me "lesbian" as an insult and did not like me. I have had a lot of people make homophobic comments toward me as well, for example when I was on a different sports team a girl made a comment that I was attracted to every girl on the team just because I was gay and that she thought it was creepy.

***

How do we stop bullying? The eternal question.

CHAPTER 23

WHAT HAS BEEN THE BIGGEST TURNING POINT TOWARD EQUALITY IN YOUR OPINION? THE STONEWALL UPRISING? THE MARRIAGE EQUALITY ACT? SOMETHING ELSE?

CORKY
76
MR.

I pretty well covered this back in #9. But as I said about "getting to know us," it was the natural progression and our community feeling strong and demanding equality that it was only a matter of time that "Marriage Equality" would become a reality! I was proud to be a speaker when we'd have demonstrations seeking, first, civil unions, then, as with our straight counterparts, the right to marry and have all the "benefits" they have!

What has been the biggest turning point toward equality in your opinion? The Stonewall Uprising? The Marriage Equality Act? Something else?

DAVID
69
HE

There have been so many. Reading about the Stonewall riots as current news had a great impact on me. Gays didn't have to be closeted, we could speak out. It still would be several years before the promise of the riots would be fully realized if they truly have been, but it offered hope.

One small turning point I was involved with was here in Denver. When my partner's first book was published, a few of our friends planned a reception for him at the Denver Botanic Gardens. The friend that was most responsible for the party was a member of The Garden Club. One of her fellow club members made the mistake of telling her later that she and many other club members were scandalized that she had a gay friend. Our friend let it be known in no uncertain terms that there was nothing scandalous about it and it was not a topic for further discussion. Soon after that, the club took a field trip to Colorado Springs. Apparently, in the van going down and coming back, the conversation was all "Rob and David this," and "Rob and David that." After that, it was almost unheard of to have a party in Cherry Creek without having some gays in attendance or at least working for the caterer. Suddenly, all the in crowd had to have a gay friend even if it was just their hairdresser. I believe that change in attitudes of Denver's high society helped change the culture of much of Denver.

JW
66

Marriage. The Marriage Equality Act.

ROB
66

I don't think it can be pinpointed, but I do think that when people welcomed Will and Grace into their living rooms, the tide had turned.

CJEAN
63
HE/HIM

The revolt against Anita Bryant's "Save Our Children" campaign in Dade County, Florida, and the backlash when it supported the Briggs Initiative—California Proposition 6 that was defeated. The murder of Harvey Milk also galvanized our community. The March on Washington also showed our numbers.

SHANNON
58

Certainly Stonewall started it all. For me, personally, the Marriage Equality Act has had the most impact. It allowed me to have parental rights to my children and to have the privileges of a spouse without having to hide all the time. People have treated me with much more respect since marriage equality passed. It makes me feel like a real citizen as opposed to someone who has to hide everything and fight for every scrap.

TOM
58

I think the Stonewall Uprising was the turning point that made possible all the gains that followed.

What has been the biggest turning point toward equality in your opinion? The Stonewall Uprising? The Marriage Equality Act? Something else?

TONY
58
HE/HIM

Each has been an important turning point. And in my lifetime, Stonewall was a critical catalyst for change. Each successive victory at the Supreme Court (Romer, Lawrence, Obergefell) all have kept momentum.

Although, I truly knew that we were on the other side when we ran into friends on our wedding day. My (now husband) and I were walking our dog and stopped to get a bagel and coffee the morning of our wedding. The caterers wanted us out of the house (we got married in our backyard in D.C.). We ran into Bill's colleague (straight) and their kids. They of course asked what we were up to that day and we said we were getting married. A week or so later, Bill got a call and she shared the story of her nine-year-old son. Upon learning that we were getting married, his reaction was, "Well, how can they be out walking the dog, don't they have things to do to get ready for their wedding?" His reaction wasn't, "Why are two men getting married?" That thought didn't cross his mind, rather he thought we would be too busy getting ready. Through tears, we realized in that moment that the world had changed.

CHRISTOPHER
57

Marriage Equality is probably what finally cemented in society's mind, that equality under the law, was irreversible.

GUS
57
HE/HIM

Nothing could happen until Stonewall or Harvey Milk happened. Bless those courageous enough to fight back and stand for equality. We stand on their shoulders.

BRAD
54

The Marriage Equality Act.

ANTHONY
53
HE/HIM/HIS

Marriage Equality.

JOHN
52
GAY MALE AND HE/HIM/HIS

In all fairness, most every generation is going to see the act that occurred in their lifetime as the biggest one. Those who lived through Stonewall saw things move the most forward for that time, even though years later everyone would come to realize that equality was still far from fully in hand. But for me, Marriage Equality is up there for gays like the Civil Rights Act hopefully is/was for POC.

MIKE
51
HE/HIM/HIS

The Marriage Equality Act.

What has been the biggest turning point toward equality in your opinion?
The Stonewall Uprising? The Marriage Equality Act? Something else?

PASHA
51
SHE/HER OR THEY/THEM

Of course, the Stonewall Uprising and the Marriage Equality Act are profound. But one of the biggest turning points for any movement is the acceptance into pop culture. When RuPaul hit it big and *Will and Grace* and *To Wong Foo* and *The Bird Cage* held a mirror to society in a non-threatening way and normalized LGBTQIA+ culture, to me was when I saw change in the general public.

DAVID
50
HE/HIM

The Marriage Equality Act is huge. Hoping to do that soon in the near future.

MICHAEL
50
HE/HIM/HIS

KIMMY
47
HIM/HER

Marriage Equality.

JONATHAN
44
HE/HIM

Wow! This is a hard one for me. I like to consider myself a student of history so I believe many events contribute to the whole. I do think that the greatest turning point for the LGBTQ+ community as relates to equality would be marriage and all the rights that that entails. But I also believe that the Stonewall Uprising provided the base on which all other steps toward LGBTQ+ equality stand on. Every event is interconnected.

JV
43
HE/HIM/HIS

It's still quite a journey, but being able to marry my husband and it being on paper is huge. The fact that some are still trying to take it away boggles my mind.

KAYTI
LOOK 32, FEEL 78, LEGALLY 42
RECENTLY FEMALE (SHE/HER/HERS) TO EVERYONE BUT BLOOD FAMILY

Pass.

RYAN
39
HE/HIM

The Marriage Equality Act.

What has been the biggest turning point toward equality in your opinion? The Stonewall Uprising? The Marriage Equality Act? Something else?

STEPHEN
38
HE/HIM

ANDREW
30
PANSEXUAL TRANSGUY—HE/HIM

That's hard to say, I think because each one, along with others, have generally made equally but different impacts on equality. Their impacts are different and some definitely helped lead the way for other events to follow. So I personally find it hard to say which one has been the biggest turning point—I'm not the best one to answer that.

JACKSON
30
HE/HIM/HIS

The Marriage Equality Act really was a turning point in my history. It was a game changer and really inspired my motivation to pursue a legal/political career.

MISS JESSICA
27
NON-BINARY, ALL PRONOUNS

Marriage Equality. I agree Stonewall has had an initial start impact, but the truth is so much of that has been forgotten and the issues still remain.

PARRISH
23
HE/HIM

MADI
21
SHE/HER

Stonewall for sure. It was the first time that the LGBTQ+ community had had enough. They fought back. They were over it, and look where we are now. Credit for this goes entirely to the black trans women that lead this movement, and I wish more people realized this, especially in the LGBTQ+ community itself.

FREYA
20
SHE/HER/HERS

I think Biden being elected as our new president was a huge turning point. Although gay marriage has been legal, there was talk of people turning that law and making it illegal once again. I think having Biden in office has made a huge difference for the community.

***

If you are not familiar with the Stonewall Uprising, Harvey Milk, or the Marriage Equality Act, I encourage you to research them. Doing so will no doubt lead you to other historical events/people like The Lavender Scare, Marsha P. Johnson and Sylvia Rivera, Ballroom Culture, the Mattachine Society, and so much more!. Educate yourself so history doesn't repeat itself.

CHAPTER 24

WHAT'S YOUR FAVORITE HASHTAG?

CORKY
76
MR.

I'm trying to "bridge the age difference" with learning new things, but hashtags are not something I'm fully aware of. LOL!

DAVID
69
HE

I don't know a hashtag from corned beef hash.

JW
66

Don't have one yet—don't understand.

ROB
66

As if.

CJEAN
63
HE/HIM

I am not on Twitter—so don't track them. I have seen many clever ones go by though.

SHANNON
58

I don't really do hashtags much. I'm old!

TOM
58

I do not really know what hashtags are, or how they work.

TONY
58
HE/HIM

#whatthehellisahashtag

CHRISTOPHER
57

#LoveIsLove

GUS
57
HE/HIM

˘

BRAD
54

I'm not much into hashtags. I guess it's my age! LOL. Hardly use them.

ANTHONY
53
HE/HIM/HIS

For sobriety: #notevenone. For life: #53andFabulous (Whatever year I'm celebrating my age).

JOHN
52
GAY MALE AND HE/HIM/HIS

Honestly, I do not have one because my favorite depends on what is happening at a particular point in time and then we all move on.

MIKE
51
HE/HIM/HIS

None.

PASHA
51
SHE/HER OR THEY/THEM

#LoveWins. I like it more than #LoveIsLove because when working with kids, LIL can be a lightening rod for detractors. Plus, I hope that in the end love more than exists. It wins.

DAVID
50
HE/HIM

#noh8

MICHAEL
50
HE/HIM/HIS

#blessed

KIMMY
47
HIM/HER

I don't pay attention to hashtags or things that are trending. I'm always late to the game regarding what's popular.

JONATHAN
44
HE/HIM

N/A

JV
43
HE/HIM/HIS

#ONELOVE

KAYTI
LOOK 32, FEEL 78, LEGALLY 42
RECENTLY FEMALE (SHE/HER/HERS) TO EVERYONE BUT BLOOD FAMILY

Pass.

RYAN
39
HE/HIM

#sorrynotsorry

STEPHEN
38
HE/HIM

ANDREW
30
PANSEXUAL TRANSGUY—HE/HIM

Admittedly not much of a user of hashtags to be honest. I get the idea behind them, I just never remember to use them or can decide which ones are the best/appropriate one at any given time.

JACKSON
30
HE/HIM/HIS

MISS JESSICA
27
NON-BINARY, ALL PRONOUNS

#sexsells

PARRISH
23
HE/HIM

MADI
21
SHE/HER

#LOVEISLOVE

FREYA
20
SHE/HER/HERS

#lovetrumpshate

***

#ILoveAllOfThese

CHAPTER 25

WHO DO YOU FEEL IS THE GREATEST LGBTQ+ ICON, WHY?

CORKY
76
MR.

The "Drag Queens" who rose up against the police at the Stonewall, definitely were "true icons"! However, as an individual, I've mentioned him before yet, in my opinion, I would nominate Harvey Milk. At a time when we had no "national leader" he was there, standing tall and inspiring us that gay people were every bit as deserving as anyone else! He "lit the fuse" to believing in ourselves and continue with a new sense of importance.

DAVID
69
HE

At the moment, Mayor Pete, for reasons that should be obvious. There are also many iconic gays and lesbians. Rachel Maddow is way up on my list. Governor Jared Polis is another as are so many mayors and other elected officials.

JW
66
Mayor Pete.

ROB
66
Cher.

CJEAN
63
HE/HIM

Accomplishment—Alan Turing. He was the turning point in WWII when he broke the Enigma Code and started modern computing.

Representation—Harvey Milk.

SHANNON
58
I don't really get into icons and celebrities too much. I would say that I am most grateful for the bravery of Harvey Milk, and Obergefell, and countless others who have fought for equality for LGBTQ people.

TOM
58
I would say Cher and Bette Midler. They are not gay, but everyone in the community seems to love them.

TONY
58
HE/HIM
Harvey Milk. If you haven't already seen it, you absolutely must watch this documentary, *The Times of Harvey Milk*.

CHRISTOPHER
57

Harvey Milk because he was a rallying figure that we so needed at the time.

GUS
57
HE/HIM

The parents of PFLAG, everywhere around the world. Nothing is as powerful as the love and embrace of a parent.

BRAD
54

Maybe Elton John. He's a huge pop rock icon, makes people happy and dance, a charitable person and very respected in the gay community, and in a long, loving relationship. There are so many people that I admire, it's hard to pick just one.

ANTHONY
53
HE/HIM/HIS

Again, we don't have just one.

JOHN
52
GAY MALE AND HE/HIM/HIS

I doubt I could narrow it down to just one. Cher, Madonna, Patty Lupone are obvious choices. Dan Savage has been pretty iconic. As has Goldie Hawn, Ryan Murphy. There are just too many to even pull up in one moment of memory.

MIKE
51
HE/HIM/HIS

None.

PASHA
51
SHE/HER OR THEY/THEM

Oh Lort! Too many for me to name! Isn't that a great problem to have?

DAVID
50
HE/HIM

I love Divine! He just didn't give a fuck! LOL.

MICHAEL
50
HE/HIM/HIS

Greg Louganis. Gay and with HIV, still navigated the world of Olympic Diving with grace and professionalism. He never gave up, always pushed harder and was one of the first recognizable advocates for LGBTQI+ people and HIV infected people around the world.

KIMMY
47
HIM/HER

JONATHAN
44
HE/HIM

Another hard one with no easy answer. There are so many I could list. Marsha P. Johnson, Harvey Milk, Slyvia Rivera, Heather Gregg Spillman, Edith Windsor, Alan Turing, Gilbert Baker, Cher, Matthew Shepard and many, many more. Most icons are local, never enjoying national recognition. As the saying goes, it takes a village.

JV
43
HE/HIM/HIS

Cher! She just loves our community so much and her support for Chaz is just beyond what a lot of us long for!

KAYTI
LOOK 32, FEEL 78, LEGALLY 42
RECENTLY FEMALE (SHE/HER/HERS) TO EVERYONE BUT BLOOD FAMILY

Pass.

RYAN
39
HE/HIM

I am really drawn to Elton John. He represents a time in history when being gay was taboo, and yet he pursued his dreams and paved a path for many in doing so.

STEPHEN
38
HE/HIM

ANDREW
30
PANSEXUAL TRANSGUY—HE/HIM

Admittedly, no idea at this time!

JACKSON
30
HE/HIM/HIS

Ellen DeGeneres, she is the first open and out celebrity lesbian.

MISS JESSICA
27
NON-BINARY, ALL PRONOUNS

N/A

PARRISH
23
HE/HIM

MADI
21
SHE/HER

Marsha P. Johnson by far. She is the reason Stonewall happened, and she accomplished so much in her lifetime.

FREYA
20
SHE/HER/HERS

I think there are many, but I love Laverne Cox. I think she is so amazing and supportive to the community. As a transgender woman today, she is strong and supportive. I saw her for the first time in the show *Orange Is the New Black* and thought she was a wonderful actress. After doing research and understanding her outward support, I knew I would love her and appreciate her as a woman.

***

So many listed—everyone from politics to historical to entertainment! They are all supportive and have in their own way advanced the moves toward equality for the LGBTQ+ community.

CHAPTER 26

HAVE YOU EXPERIENCED INEQUALITY IN HEALTHCARE BECAUSE YOU ARE LGBTQ+? WHAT HAPPENED?

CORKY
76
MR.

No, again. Luckily, I've never experienced inequality in healthcare.

DAVID
69
HE

No, I haven't. I met a gay doctor in Denver when I was living in Fort Collins. He was my doctor until he retired. I found another gay-friendly practice and I've been with them since then.

JW
66

I have not experienced any inequality with a healthcare professional.

ROB
66

No.

CJEAN
63
HE/HIM

Only that I confused my doctor when I had to tell him I was in a same sex relationship. I only sought community recommended providers to receive knowledgable care.

SHANNON
58

Not really, but the birth of our son sort of relates to this. Because there was no marriage equality at the time of his birth, we had to jump through a lot of hoops for me to get parental rights. We found out through mutual friends that if he was born in a state where we were legally married, I would be listed as a parent on the birth certificate. We decided to have the baby in Washington, D.C. (about a five-hour drive from our home in North Carolina). We made a trip in October and got married and met with an OBGYN who was willing to work with us through the process. We arrived in D.C. three weeks before the due date and stayed at a friend's condo for a week and then at one of my parents' timeshares until the baby was born. It was absolutely miserable. We waited forever. Jenny was in labor for three days. Our time at the timeshare was about to run out. We didn't know what we were going to do. Once he was born, we had one more day at the timeshare. We loaded up and drove back to NC in a snowstorm. It got so bad we had to stop at a hotel. There were no rooms left and the people in front of us in line gave us their room since we had a newborn baby.

We didn't have to go through any of that with our daughter. Marriage equality had passed, so she was born three miles from our house. My name is on her birth certificate, though I'm listed as "father." My lawyer says I'm all legal.

TOM
58

Never. Our physician is a wonderfully kind man. He knows we're gay, and it doesn't matter to him in the slightest.

TONY
58
HE/HIM

No.

CHRISTOPHER
57

No, I've personally never experienced inequality in healthcare.

GUS
57
HE/HIM

None that I can pinpoint.

BRAD
54

I really truly haven't. I feel some doctors haven't known exactly how to relate to me as a gay patient, but not discriminated against. I feel

I've been fortunate, a human with feelings and emotions and supported, especially as a spouse of someone who was going through an extremely difficult, life-changing experience when my husband was passing away. We both were treated wonderful by the medical community in the town we lived.

ANTHONY
53
HE/HIM/HIS

No.

JOHN
52
GAY MALE AND HE/HIM/HIS

No.

MIKE
51
HE/HIM/HIS

No.

PASHA
51
SHE/HER OR THEY/THEM

I would say the denial of access to PReP by a GP or OB/GYN qualifies. Children can get the HPV shot with no problem to prevent an STD/STI. So, why do you have to go to a disease specialist to get Truvada? Even then, you feel the stigma and judgment from doctors. I go to Planned Parenthood where I don't feel the sting of condemnation from providers.

DAVID
50
HE/HIM

Not really because of being gay. I just had a bad doctor in the past.

MICHAEL
50
HE/HIM/HIS

I have not, fortunately.

KIMMY
47
HIM/HER

No.

JONATHAN
44
HE/HIM

Never experienced healthcare inequality due to being LGBTQ+.

JV
43
HE/HIM/HIS

Thankfully no. And hoping we never have to.

KAYTI
LOOK 32, FEEL 78, LEGALLY 42
RECENTLY FEMALE (SHE/HER/HERS) TO EVERYONE BUT BLOOD FAMILY

I am actively dealing with collections and insurance over about $400 as the blood work required to check estrogen and testosterone levels were not covered.

RYAN
39
HE/HIM

I have not.

STEPHEN
38
HE/HIM

ANDREW
30
PANSEXUAL TRANSGUY—HE/HIM

I have struggled with healthcare in regards to being scared about being misunderstood or for basic needs not being met after it's been discovered that I'm trans and the whole thing zeroing in on that instead of what I came in for. Or worse, if they choose to refuse me because I am trans. I do rationally know that being trans is a part of my healthcare, I just don't want it to be the defining thing for my healthcare unnecessarily, however that manifests. With that being said, I've found a supportive doctor to support that I am trans along with all other health concerns that are not related to that aspect of me.

JACKSON
30
HE/HIM/HIS

No.

MISS JESSICA
27
NON-BINARY, ALL PRONOUNS

Not inequality, however I have experienced lack of compassion and love from people in healthcare when asking questions about my sex life, my pronouns, etc.

PARRISH
23
HE/HIM

MADI
21
SHE/HER

Personally, I have not.

FREYA
20
SHE/HER/HERS

No, I have not. I am going into the healthcare field with my degree from college and am interested to see how that pans out.

***

Still an area that needs more training and equality.

CHAPTER 27

DESCRIBE THE FIRST TIME YOU FELT TRULY HAPPY AFTER COMING OUT.

CORKY
76
MR.

Living in San Francisco, there were several times I did feel happy, mostly feeling a "sense of unity" at mammoth Halloween celebrations or political rallies, and celebrating when Harvey Milk became the very first "openly gay man" elected to a position of esteem in any city! After returning to Denver in '83, I didn't go out to any gay bars, clubs or any other places for many years. In 1998, I did go to a bar, The Triangle, one night to find out there was dancing...I was elated! Unfortunately, I had a "falling out" with a (supposedly) good friend, so I stopped going out again until 2005 when a guy I had met, asked if I'd like to go dancing. I jumped at the chance, "Of Course!" That started the most happy and rewarding phase of my life! Here I was, 61 years old, yet I had never experienced such acceptance with smiles, hugs, and so much love showered on me! This has continued right up to today when I am basking in so much caring love! When I came close to losing my life in a house fire (Aug. '16), the outpouring of concern and well wishes still brings tears to my eyes!

This part is supposed to be about the "happiest I've felt after coming out," however, one of the saddest times of my life should also be touched on, because it is completely a "gay memory." All of our jubilation of having Harvey Milk become a national figure, it shook us to the core when he was assassinated in 1978. To an individual, the sorrow and despair was almost too much to bear. The "Candle Light Vigil" down Market Street from Castro Street to City Hall will always bring me to tears. There is a slight incline up to Castro, and as you looked back, all you could see was the mass of glowing lights, totally silent, without a sound, other than the slow drum beats. I wasn't very close to Harvey, however, being a SF street artist, I was an associate of Mayor Moscone who was also slain. :'-(

DAVID
69
HE

Probably when I got over being referred to as "she" and realized that it was fine.

JW
66

I just felt like I didn't have to worry any more about how I felt or being told that I didn't belong in society. A weight was lifted off my shoulders.

ROB
66

I wasn't unhappy before so no answer.

CJEAN
63
HE/HIM

I was not miserable before coming out. It's not a panacea to fix every-thing—just a step in realizing yourself. Every step in coming out was a positive and forward moving moment. I could never relate to the self-hating fag stereotype. Closet cases are our biggest repository of hate. If they hate us, be suspicious of them and call it out—what are you hiding?

SHANNON
58

My wedding.

TOM
58

I don't know that there was a first time. I do know that the second I came out to my parents, I felt an enormous sense of relief, as if a huge weight had been lifted off my shoulders.

TONY
58
HE/HIM

I've always been pretty happy. Not sure I can think of anything par-ticular. I did feel enormous relief after coming out. And, after coming out to my family, the weight of it all was lifted. No longer could it be used against me.

CHRISTOPHER
57

The first time I felt truly happy was meeting my first love. I was 28.

GUS
57
HE/HIM

My first true loving relationship with another man. It took a while, but after "kissing a few frogs" and making a few mistakes, I found the ultimate happiness, like never before.

BRAD
54

Meeting my first husband and knowing what falling in love with another man truly felt like.

ANTHONY
53
HE/HIM/HIS

After my mom told my dad and he said he didn't care. I was his son and he loved me.

JOHN
52
GAY MALE AND HE/HIM/HIS

The immediate one and then many others. Again, I cannot answer this specific of a question because the journey was long and filled with tremendous highs and lows of equal magnitude to be honest.

MIKE
51
HE/HIM/HIS

Making out with the guy after telling him I was gay. I instantly knew who I was.

PASHA
51
SHE/HER OR THEY/THEM

My experiences kissing women at airports. For some reason it feels
extra freeing.

DAVID
50
HE/HIM

I didn't really feel any different. Just felt more of a relief after I told
everyone. I was already happy.

MICHAEL
50
HE/HIM/HIS

At Pridefest 1993 and I had just moved to Denver. It was the first
time I had experienced such a large group of publicly open people in
my life. I knew I was home.

KIMMY
47
HIM/HER

Going full drag to a nightclub and feeling included. I wasn't treated
special nor was I treated like a freak. I was just treated with respect
and got to dance with all sorts of peeps.

JONATHAN
44
HE/HIM

There are many times I felt happiness after coming out but the pinnacle would have to be twenty years later when I married my husband.

JV
43
HE/HIM/HIS

It was on our wedding day.

KAYTI
LOOK 32, FEEL 78, LEGALLY 42
RECENTLY FEMALE (SHE/HER/HERS) TO EVERYONE BUT BLOOD FAMILY

The smile while dressed hopefully sums it up.

RYAN
39
HE/HIM

I think that just the sense of relief after not having to carry that weight/burden created an ongoing happiness.

STEPHEN
38
HE/HIM

Carnegie Hall.

ANDREW
30
PANSEXUAL TRANSGUY—HE/HIM

I would say when I started hearing people use my pronouns and name, especially in public by those who don't know me personally.

JACKSON
30
HE/HIM/HIS

The first time I felt truly happy after coming out was getting my legal name/gender marker changed. The feeling was indescribable!

MISS JESSICA
27
NON-BINARY, ALL PRONOUNS

Something I am still working on 4.5 years later.

PARRISH
23
HE/HIM

The second I came out to the most important people of my life, just so they knew, regardless of what they thought. And then from there, I came out to the whole world as in friends from high school, family out of state, new college friends, etc. I just dropped a picture with the guy I was seeing on Instagram and had no worries.

MADI
21
SHE/HER

I felt truly happy on the night of my senior prom with my girl-friend by my side for the first time in a really public and exposed situation. The amount of support we received from our classmates was incredible.

FREYA
20
SHE/HER/HERS

When I was able to go out with my girlfriend and not hide the fact that we were dating and happy together.

***

Marrying! Acceptance! Being yourself in public! All the things mentioned are what any of us want. However, you shouldn't have to work for them the way that the LGBTQ+ community has to.

CHAPTER 28

HOW DO YOU FEEL ABOUT STRAIGHT PEOPLE COMING TO LGBTQ+ EVENTS, NIGHT CLUBS, SHOWS ETC.?

CORKY
76
MR.

There are many gays who are not pleased with straight people coming to "our bars, clubs and events," but I have no objection, for the most part. I do want everyone to be able to party and relax around everyone else, and I'm thrilled when I see more and more straights coming to party with us! "They," especially the women, know that "we" do know how to have a good time and I appreciate it when their men friends are not bothered to be around gay men. However, there can be a drawback as I've noticed at Tracks! It was always a gay club and straights were welcome, but with the changing demographics in Lodo, so many young people are moving into that area. Before COVID changed everything, on any given Saturday night, there were as many, if not more straights there, and the mood seemed to have changed. Still lots of gays, yet "we" were almost made to feel it was a "Str8 dance venue" and gays were tolerated! So many "regulars" stopped going there!

DAVID
69
HE

I've never encouraged it, but I have done it, mainly with family members. I've seldom been bothered by it. It has hacked me off when straight women think it's fun to go into the bathrooms so they can watch guys pee. A little decorum please.

JW
66

I have no problems as long as they are there to enjoy and have fun without causing any problems.

ROB
66

Fine. I have been resentful in the past of clubs where the straight people came as tourists. We are not exhibits.

CJEAN
63
HE/HIM

I love our allies—my favorite group in a Pride Parade was always PFLAG. I absolutely hated it when straight girls decided taking over a gay bar for their bridal shower was a "thing." BLM talks about cultural appropriation and it is the same thing. When we only had our safe spaces to be, it felt awful to have them overwhelmed by those who wanted to display how accepting they were, rather than be an asset to our community. Lesbians had straight men in their spaces looking for a three way—those were particularly disgusting.

SHANNON
58

I am fine with straight people attending events. I don't really go to that stuff any more. Too busy raising a family.

TOM
58

I think it's great; however, I'm not a fan of women at gay bars, but the times are changing, which is probably a good thing.

TONY
58
HE/HIM

It is great to have support and allies. For truly public events, it is really critical for allies to show their support. I do think sometimes it's nice and important to have a safe space. Think of the Pulse night-club. That horrific event also shed light on the importance of having a safe place to be who you are. For some of the victims, they "came out" to their parents and family members when they were informed they had been murdered. I am grateful for the comfort and safety in my life that I can be out wherever I go. So, while I might not "need" a gay bar, the need still exists. When I was coming out, the safety and camaraderie at my local gay bar was really important. I think that need still exists today, and when allies want to visit, they might want to keep in mind they are guests in a sacred space.

CHRISTOPHER
57

I am all for it as long as it is to be a part of the celebration!

GUS
57
HE/HIM

As long as they come as allies and not exploiters, I say "great."

BRAD
54

It's fine, but I feel some people treat it like it's a novelty. I think those days are over, as the LGBTQ+ community is more accepted. But, back in the day, I felt like sometimes straight people were going to gay bars/clubs/events to stare and observe gay people.

ANTHONY
53
HE/HIM/HIS

We are one community.

JOHN
52
GAY MALE AND HE/HIM/HIS

I mean, we need allies and we should welcome them and they should be welcome. But often it gets muddled and our spaces can run the risk of losing themselves. While I appreciate all that our allies do, sometimes you just want to be gay.

MIKE
51
HE/HIM/HIS

It's great...except for drunk girls with long hair flipping around and sticking to you dancing because you're shirtless...the worst!

PASHA
51
SHE/HER OR THEY/THEM

I don't have any problem with it as long as the element of being a specifically LGBTQIA+ environment isn't the focus in an exploitative feeling way. (Is that even a word?) Like going to the zoo to gawk at animals.

DAVID
50
HE/HIM

I'm perfectly fine with it. A lot of my friends are straight.

MICHAEL
50
HE/HIM/HIS

I love the camaraderie, fellowship and allies I have grown to know and love. We are all humans last time I checked. We should all be allowed to participate in the human experience together and learn from each other. How else can we grow?

KIMMY
47
HIM/HER

I don't really care one way or another. Since more straight people attend these events, I suppose it shows that many people don't care about orientation either and are simply hoping to have fun. In my limited experience, the clubs or events that have a cover charge or sell tickets are less aggravating because "haters" are not going to pay so they can provoke lgbt people. (You wouldn't buy a ticket to see a band just to go boo them.)

JONATHAN
44
HE/HIM

The more the merrier. Inclusion means everyone.

JV
43
HE/HIM/HIS

I love it. As long as it's to support and be allies, I'm all for it.

KAYTI
LOOK 32, FEEL 78, LEGALLY 42
*RECENTLY FEMALE (SHE/HER/HERS) TO EVERYONE BUT
BLOOD FAMILY*

I am fine with it if they understand etiquette. Not like "Hey girl," but how to be cordial and if you spill a drink on someone, not to tuck tail and take off into the crowd.

RYAN
39
HE/HIM

I think it's great! It is wonderful to have allies! And again, everyone has a place at the table.

STEPHEN
38
HE/HIM

I love it if they know they're there as an ally in our safe place, not making it their own space. I want straight people to feel as comfortable around us as much as anyone else, as if it's a non-issue (because it is). So, where better to start that kind of integration.

242

ANDREW
30
PANSEXUAL TRANSGUY—HE/HIM

It depends on the situation. As a general rule, no I don't have a problem with straight people coming to these events, such as pride or something, especially if it's in support of a friend(s) or family member(s). With that being said, there are things, events and such where I would say it is inappropriate for a straight, cisgender person to go. For example, I know there are support groups for trans people by trans people to support each other; this would be an inappropriate place for a cisgender person to be (except for the rare occasion they are invited because perhaps they are a doctor who tends to trans healthcare needs in some way; but the key is this individual is invited to be at this specific event/meeting). I would say it would be something to those who are allies to be mindful of. There are LGTBQ events and places that you are welcome to go to but there are some sacred places that are our own and be respectful of that. If you don't know, simply and respectfully just ask and accept whatever the answer is.

JACKSON
30
HE/HIM/HIS

I love seeing people of all walks of life being able to enjoy one another. I just believe in being friendly to all.

MISS JESSICA
27
NON-BINARY, ALL PRONOUNS

I absolutely love it! There just needs to be awareness when you enter a safe space not necessarily for you.

PARRISH
23
HE/HIM

I think it really depends on why they are going. I love bringing some of my friends to LGBTQ+ events, clubs, etc. because I enjoy them, and I want them to experience it. I don't always use it as a way to "educate" them, rather I just want to have fun with the community I am in and hope my friends will have fun too. If people are going for the wrong reasons, then it makes me upset because you don't need to be there unless you are going to be open-minded to it.

MADI
21
SHE/HER

I am fine with them coming, so long as they are there with someone who is part of the community. Pride is different, I am mostly talking about clubs. They must realize also that they are a guest here, and that this is not their space to get trashed in and make a fool of themselves.

FREYA
20
SHE/HER/HERS

I think it is wonderful that those of other beliefs and communities support others. I appreciate it and would never bash on someone for showing support. I do not like when straight people think they have the right to call themselves an "honorary gay" or think just because they have a few gay friends that they are the same and go through the same things. I think people need to understand their place when it comes to supporting and being a part of these events.

How do you feel about straight people coming to LGBTQ+ events, night clubs, shows etc.? The Stonewall Uprising? The Marriage Equality Act? Something else? 200

***

If you're hetero, you are a guest—be respectful. I have witnessed the bachelorette parties that get out of hand and act like they are the only ones who matter and it is so wrong. I know several people who own/manage gay bars and I still don't go unless I am with someone from the community.

CHAPTER 29

WHAT IS THE DUMBEST QUESTION YOU HAVE BEEN ASKED?

CORKY
76
MR.

Dumbest question... "How do you know you're gay?" Duh. I've had to say, "How do you know you're straight"?

DAVID
69
HE

"How do two guys do it?"

JW
66

If I play the man or the woman in the marriage. Or is there a role we play? Or do I play a specific role?

ROB
66

I'm sure I've forgotten them.

CJEAN
63
HE/HIM

College fraternity/sorority: "Are you gay? What a waste."
Response: "Oh honey—it ain't being wasted."

SHANNON
58

Where did you get your kids? Like I bought them at a store or something.

TOM
58

Who's the woman in your relationship?

TONY
58
HE/HIM

Who is the man (or woman) in your relationship?

CHRISTOPHER
57

Dumbest question? No such thing as long as it is sincere.

GUS
57
HE/HIM

Are you two brothers?

BRAD
54

Are you two brothers? and, Who's the man and who's the woman in your house?

ANTHONY
53
HE/HIM/HIS

JOHN
52
GAY MALE AND HE/HIM/HIS

MIKE
51
HE/HIM/HIS

Who's the wife?

PASHA
51
SHE/HER OR THEY/THEM

"Is your vagina only half slanted because you're only half Asian?" He was totally serious.

DAVID
50
HE/HIM

Are you sure you're not straight? Lol.

MICHAEL
50
HE/HIM/HIS

When in drag... Do I want to be a woman? Gays are allowed to express themselves and drag is just that for me, an artistic expression.

KIMMY
47
HIM/HER

Do I think that God approves of me wearing nail polish and cross-dressing? My reply... When I die, God is going to ask me if I fed the hungry and if I helped those in need and I'm certain he won't be asking about my nail polish. I also said that when I die he won't be asking me about your sins, he will be asking me about mine—which was my subtle and nice way of saying mind your business.

JONATHAN
44
HE/HIM

N/A

JV
43
HE/HIM/HIS

Do you have AIDS? Ugh! Not recently, but back in the day.

KAYTI
LOOK 32, FEEL 78, LEGALLY 42
RECENTLY FEMALE (SHE/HER/HERS) TO EVERYONE BUT BLOOD FAMILY

Pass.

RYAN
39
HE/HIM

I think when people come out and ask about your sexual preferences, it is not only dumb, but highly inappropriate (and it happens often).

STEPHEN
38
HE/HIM

ANDREW
30
PANSEXUAL TRANSGUY—HE/HIM

Cannot think of what's necessarily the dumbest question, but some of the most inappropriate question(s) that people can't seem to understand why they are super personal are—What's in your pants? How do you have sex?

JACKSON
30
HE/HIM/HIS

No question is dumb if asked. If people genuinely want to learn a topic, I am privy to, I never mind answering.

MISS JESSICA
27
NON-BINARY, ALL PRONOUNS

How do you know if you're gay? You've never had sex with "insert other gender."

PARRISH
23
HE/HIM

MADI
21
SHE/HER

"Who wears the pants in your relationship?" Fuck off.

FREYA
20
SHE/HER/HERS

Who acts more like the guy in the relationship?

***

The questions listed are completely inappropriate. Straight people don't get asked such personal questions. If you do have a question, find the right time and place to ask it with respect and honesty.

CHAPTER 30

HAVE YOU EXPERIENCED DISCRIMINATION WITHIN THE COMMUNITY?

CORKY
76
MR.

During my early years in San Francisco, I did feel discrimination directed at me. Mostly because I didn't "fit the gay mold" at the dance clubs, which were pretty "cliquey"! My hair was longer than theirs, I felt the music which "moved me," when they barely raised their hands. Some of them would actually turn up their noses at me! Fortunately, being such a "little one" my entire life, I was used to people giving me a second look, but never with this obvious disapproval! I can remember my mom saying, when people would act in ways that were inappropriate or uncalled for, "Just be happy. You're not that way." Or, "Let it go, like water on a duck's back." It was about that time, I "found" my craft, became a street artist and never let it bother me again!

That was the only time I felt discrimination, but I know it does exist in todays's GLBTQ+, mostly aimed at drag queens and transgender members. Of course, I think it's unnecessary and cruel, but for the most part, we do get along as a family.

DAVID
69
HE

Denver and especially places like Capitol Hill and northwest Denver are cool. Where I grew up, you could be killed for being or appearing to be gay and there would be no legal repercussions. At least, it could get you punched in the mouth.

JW
66

I have never been in any situation where I felt I had been discriminated against. My employers have been very open to it.

ROB
66

No.

CJEAN
63
HE/HIM

Oh yes. Queens are like other humans and could be vicious at times. There were so many cliques—A-Gays, GymRats, Butch, StraightActing, Fashion, Age, Appearance. We all had to find our place we felt comfortable. I always avoided the "A-Group" like the plague, and was much happier referencing myself in the B or C group.

SHANNON
58

I'm not really in the community since moving to CO. We don't know anybody like us here. I have not experienced overt discrimination, it's usually subtle. An example would be friends from my past don't really talk to me anymore. Or a weird look when people realize I'm gay.

TOM
58

Sometimes young guys behave badly toward older men. Youth is pushed down our throats just as it is in hetero society.

TONY
58
HE/HIM

Discrimination? Hmmm. Not really. When working on the ordinance, we were holding a fundraiser at a local gay bar. A gay patron approached me and said, "Why are you doing this? You should stop! You are bringing too much attention to us." I was quite shocked. I retorted, "Well, I am doing this for me and those who want these rights. I am sorry that you don't. That's your problem, and not mine."

Infighting, oh yes. Every minority group experiences infighting. When Amendment 2 passed in Colorado, those of us who had been involved in the fight were castigated quite publicly in some instances. I still bear many a "stab wound" in the back. It is important to recognize, as with straight people, the LGBTQ+ community is not a monolith. We are not all friends with one another. Not one person can speak for the community as there are so many different perspectives and life experiences.

CHRISTOPHER
57

I haven't really experienced discrimination within the community, but I have seen others affected by it, unfortunately. No group is immune.

GUS
57
HE/HIM

I think that guys who have "always known they were gay" and have lived in the gay community their whole lives can look down on those of us who took our time figuring it out...especially those of us with kids.

BRAD
54

No, not really. In some places I've lived, I feel that the trans community has tried to "hijack" the LGBTQ+ community, I guess you could say. Making the community more about them than equally about all of us. It's not a competition—we're all in this together. We're all the human race—our diversity as people is what makes us special and unique.

ANTHONY
53
HE/HIM/HIS

I have not firsthand, but we easily talk trash about one another behind each other's backs. Again, it's hiding behind a computer keyboard.

JOHN
52
GAY MALE AND HE/HIM/HIS

Probably.

MIKE
51
HE/HIM/HIS

Not really, but it can be cliquey.

PASHA
51
SHE/HER OR THEY/THEM

All the time! My partner and I are both queer with long-term (years long) same gender relationships. But he's cis-male and I'm cis-female so somehow our queerness is called into question.

DAVID
50
HE/HIM

Yes, especially as you get older. Young pretentious twinks can be vicious. Lol.

MICHAEL
50
HE/HIM/HIS

I absolutely have experienced discrimination within our own communities. Sometimes, I feel that we are so worried that associating with other facets might "rub off," or we might lose our identity or heaven forbid any masculinity we've strived for if we mingle. Internal discrimination is to our detriment.

KIMMY
47
HIM/HER

Yes. Ageism at a popular gay bar on Colfax whose name starts with a C. They were all smiles and happy to take my cover charge, but I was completely ignored by the bartenders. I never did get a drink. I left over an hour later, after attempting to get served at four of their bar areas.

JONATHAN
44
HE/HIM

I consider myself one of the lucky ones. I haven't experienced out-
right discrimination within the community. Though I would be naive
to think that it doesn't exist. I mean you hear such horror stories of
discrimination on apps like Grindr. As with most discrimination, I
can't believe we have to keep talking about it in the year 2021.

JV
43
HE/HIM/HIS

Not a whole lot, but sometimes as a gay male you feel discriminated
against because you don't have the washboard abs, etc.

KAYTI
LOOK 32, FEEL 78, LEGALLY 42
*RECENTLY FEMALE (SHE/HER/HERS) TO EVERYONE BUT
BLOOD FAMILY*

Inherent bias, yes, but I don't think active denial/discrimination.

RYAN
39
HE/HIM

I have not been on the receiving end of discrimination, but I know
that it is very prevalent in the gay world...especially among gay men.
White, muscular, attractive men seem to dominate the gay world,
and I have witnessed several times in which gay men of color have
been discriminated against by other gay men.

STEPHEN
38
HE/HIM

Yes.

ANDREW
30
PANSEXUAL TRANSGUY—HE/HIM

I personally have not, but that doesn't mean it can't happen somewhere within the community.

JACKSON
30
HE/HIM/HIS

Sure, some gay men and lesbians find it hard to understand transitioning. Also, some lesbians feel they are the same as transmen. I have seen some divisions displayed inside of the community.

MISS JESSICA
27
NON-BINARY, ALL PRONOUNS

All the damn time.

PARRISH
23
HE/HIM

As a gay man, the "discrimination," I would say, is about who is better, who looks better, who knows more gay friends, who can be the top gay. I know it seems minuscule compared to other things, but there is almost a stereotype of how you need to be the "perfect" gay. If you do not match that view, you are less than other gays in a way.

MADI
21
SHE/HER

I wish that nightclubs did more to encompass things for gay women/ trans individuals, as it is very much centered around white gay men. There is a lot of work to be done in this sense.

FREYA
20
SHE/HER/HERS

I have faced discrimination from others because of my sexuality, but not directly from the community.

***

This question was suggested by one of my advisors on this project and the answers make me sad.

CHAPTER 31

IS THERE SOMETHING YOU WOULD LIKE TO SAY TO STRAIGHT PEOPLE?

CORKY
76
MR.

Say to the straights? Basically what I've said lots in this "rambling." LOL. Please don't judge "us," take your time, get to know that, for the most part, we're the same as you, with the same qualities, love of family and our country. We're not, like you, going to push our sexuality in public (rather than, maybe, holding hands and a quick kiss)! When you've "opened the door," you'll probably be surprised at how fun, funny and lovable we are, and how we'll be at the head of the line when others need help! Also, thanks for opening your doors and hearts, we sincerely appreciate the opportunity to be ourselves...the closet was getting too cramped! ;-)

DAVID
69
HE

I don't care about anyone's sexuality unless they're interested in sex with me. If that's not in the cards, worry about your own love life and stop taking an interest in mine. Just how far in the closet are you?

JW
66

In your marriage, do you play the male or female role. There is no role playing; what I do with my husband behind closed doors is our story, not for everyone else to know. I don't go around asking what they do in bed or at home.

ROB
66

No. I have no great wisdom.

CJEAN
63
HE/HIM

Thank you to those with the insight to support us. Ask me anything—I can help with ignorance by dispelling untruths.

SHANNON
58

I'm just like you. Chill out! I don't want to sleep with you or turn you gay! Find something more important to worry about. I am not a threat to your way of living.

TOM
58

We're just like you, no more, no less.

TONY
58
HE/HIM

Check your privilege. Consider seeing the world through the eyes of someone who is not straight. Be sensitive to your hetero-centric approach to everything. Don't assume people you meet are straight. Notice how the world assumes "straight" and do your part to help change the narrative.

CHRISTOPHER
57
What I would say to straight people is that we are not that different.

GUS
57
HE/HIM
Love is Love.

BRAD
54
Value and treasure each other's differences. The planet would be a very boring place if we were all exactly alike.

ANTHONY
53
HE/HIM/HIS
Thank you for supporting us, thank you for being an ally to me.

JOHN
52
GAY MALE AND HE/HIM/HIS
Probably.

MIKE
51
HE/HIM/HIS
No.

PASHA
51
SHE/HER OR THEY/THEM

We aren't worse than you. We aren't better than you. We're peers and are human and make mistakes, but it's all okay. Even LGBTQIA+ kids. Be the adults to these kids you needed in your life when you struggled with something in your childhood or youth.

DAVID
50
HE/HIM

That we just want to be accepted as we are. Also, just because I'm gay does not mean that I am attracted to all men.

MICHAEL
50
HE/HIM/HIS

Be patient...we've been patient with you for years.

KIMMY
47
HIM/HER

Nothing in particular. I talk to everyone and don't care who is straight or gay. They are just people. Some are nice people and some are not. That is how it goes.

JONATHAN
44
HE/HIM

I love you. Without you, we in the LGBTQ+ community wouldn't be here. Thank you for being our allies. Unless you are the straight people that are homophobic, to you I say, go stuff yourself and I hope you choke.

JV
43
HE/HIM/HIS

Do your research about our community and what we stand for. Be an ally and by god if your child shows any little chance of just being different, embrace them and let them know you support them. We've lost so many to their family not accepting them and this needs to stop immediately!

KAYTI
LOOK 32, FEEL 78, LEGALLY 42
RECENTLY FEMALE (SHE/HER/HERS) TO EVERYONE BUT BLOOD FAMILY

Be kind.

RYAN
39
HE/HIM

If you have not walked a day in someone from the LGBTQ+ community's shoes, then keep your opinions to yourself.

STEPHEN
38
HE/HIM

ANDREW
30
PANSEXUAL TRANSGUY—HE/HIM

I would say one of the most important things as someone who is not a part of the community is to listen to those of us who are part of the community. How can you speak for us as someone who is not one of us, if you don't listen to us? Questions are welcomed generally as long as they are asked respectfully and the answer is listened to respectfully as well! This is our community, not yours, please respect that; we love allies that are respectful to us. If you're not respectful to us, you're not our ally. With that, if you make a mistake, own up to it and learn from it! It's okay to make a mistake and/or not know something/everything. But that is why it's important to listen and respectfully ask questions. Allies are never perfect, but it's important to strive to be the best you can be! Even as a member of the community myself, I am not a perfect member of it nor do I know everything about it either, so I don't expect you to be. Listen and don't argue!

JACKSON
30
HE/HIM/HIS

Compassion and love goes a long way.

MISS JESSICA
27
NON-BINARY, ALL PRONOUNS

You cannot claim being an ally. It is something that is gifted to you, continue to do your part to support humanity and love.

PARRISH
23
HE/HIM

Stop asking if I'm a top or a bottom, like why in the world do you need to know?

MADI
21
SHE/HER

This message is specifically to straight women: Guess what Susan, just because I am gay does not mean I am instantly attracted to you.

FREYA
20
SHE/HER/HERS

I would like to say to straight people that we are the same. Treat us the same. Love us the same. Act the same. We are all one and loved and just because my sexuality is different than yours does not mean I am any lesser than you.

***

Respect. Listen. Learn.

CHAPTER 32

IS THERE A QUESTION YOU THINK SHOULD BE ON THIS LIST BUT ISN'T?

CORKY
76
MR.

No additions, I think you've covered everything so thoroughly. :-)

DAVID
69
HE

JW
66

Were you ever approached by any clergymen? I wasn't; even though I went to a parochial school. Growing up, were you ever approached by an adult figure to do something sexual that you didn't want to do or know was not cool?

ROB
66

Yes. At what age did you have your first gay experience? And how was it?

CJEAN
63
HE/HIM

You have been pretty extensive, but I know I will think of something as soon as I hit Send.

SHANNON
58

TOM
58

Not that I can think of.

TONY
58
HE/HIM

If you could choose to be straight, would you?—Absolutely not. I think it's a privilege to be gay. Imagine if you believed in reincarnation. Your first life was as a straight person and if you do well enough, you might advance and return as a gay person. ;)

CHRISTOPHER
57

One question I would add is, "Do you think that allies are important, and why?" (Parasol Patrol).

GUS
57
HE/HIM

BRAD
54

Who is the most influential friend of the LGBTQ+ community in your life? I would have to say you, Heather. I admire you and your ability to bring joy and security to those in the LGBTQ+ community of Denver and Colorado. I thank you from the bottom of my heart.

ANTHONY
53
HE/HIM/HIS

JOHN
52
GAY MALE AND HE/HIM/HIS

Probably.

MIKE
51
HE/HIM/HIS

No.

PASHA
51
SHE/HER OR THEY/THEM

You're pretty darn thorough! Right now my brainmeats splodey! Ask me in a couple of days. Haha!

DAVID
50
HE/HIM

Nope, great questions!

MICHAEL
50
HE/HIM/HIS

KIMMY
47
HIM/HER

Something about monogamy versus hookup culture.

JONATHAN
44
HE/HIM

N/A

JV
43
HE/HIM/HIS

No.

KAYTI
LOOK 32, FEEL 78, LEGALLY 42
RECENTLY FEMALE (SHE/HER/HERS) TO EVERYONE BUT BLOOD FAMILY

Pass.

RYAN
39
HE/HIM

No.

STEPHEN
38
HE/HIM

ANDREW
30
PANSEXUAL TRANSGUY—HE/HIM

Could perhaps expand more in the trans community?

JACKSON
30
HE/HIM/HIS

MISS JESSICA
27
NON-BINARY, ALL PRONOUNS

I would love to see a question about physical presentation of the body, body dysmorphia, etc.

PARRISH
23
HE/HIM

MADI
21
SHE/HER

Not that I can think of.

FREYA
20
SHE/HER/HERS

***

Some awesome suggestions here... maybe a follow-up book is in order.

CHAPTER 33

A FINAL THOUGHT...

CORKY
76
MR.

I so thank you for taking on this project and writing a book!

DAVID
69
HE

I feel so lucky to have witnessed the changes in society's attitudes. As a child, I had no role models. People coming out today have so many: politicians, musicians, actors, CEOs, athletes and others. That is such an encouraging sign. I hope this helps many young people from going through the shame and loneliness I felt as a child.

JW
66

If I had to do my life over, I probably wouldn't have done too much different. Sometimes I feel bad (guilty) that I didn't have an offspring to bring into the world for my parents to love and cherish.

ROB
66

I think that perhaps being part of a minority has helped me to empathize with other minority groups. I understand their struggles and stand with them. I support Planned Parenthood, voting rights groups, BLM, conservation groups, immigrants, and any cause that seeks universal equal rights and justice.

CJEAN
63
HE/HIM

Never judge anyone on superficial items—you never know what their story is unless you ask.

SHANNON
58

TOM
58

Thank God for you, Heather. I am honored to know you. I wish I had met you about 40 years ago. You do so much good for so many in this community. You are a treasure. Thank you for writing this book.

TONY
58
HE/HIM

While the LGBTQ+ community has made significant gains, there is a long way to go. It is still okay to fire someone because they are gay. The demonization of gays by Republicans (yes, their platform still advances marriage as between a man and woman and they are

A final thought...

The Stonewall Uprising? The Marriage Equality Act? Something else?   200

behind all of the anti-trans and anti-gay legislation) will not abate until there is a major reckoning in that party (I say this as a former Republican, too). We haven't really touched on the tragic suicide rate among LGBTQ+ youth (I still think 30% or more, higher than for the non-LGBTQ population) and the small-mindedness of so much of America and the religious institutions that bear responsibility. And, how about those places on the planet where being gay is punishable by death. Yes, I have many a soapbox on which I can jump, but will refrain.

Thank you for taking on this book. I am eager to learn more about the why and how you will know you have helped make the planet a little safer for the LGBTQ+ community.

CHRISTOPHER
57

My only final thought is appreciation for what you are doing!

GUS
57
HE/HIM

You may say I'm a dreamer
But I'm not the only one.
I hope someday you'll join us
And the world will be as one.

BRAD
54

I love my life, my husband, my friends and my family. I'm a believer in reincarnation and past lives, and I must have done something really good in the past to be as blessed as I am in this life. Life. Is. Good.

ANTHONY
53
HE/HIM/HIS

Really great questions, I wish you much success as you compile all the answers. Thank you for asking for my thoughts. Hugs!

JOHN
52
GAY MALE AND HE/HIM/HIS

Thanks for asking me to participate.

Homosexuality for me has been a tremendously personal, deep, wild, terrifying but ultimately immensely rewarding experience. No life, gay, straight or otherwise, is all a bed of roses and I am confident that though the thorns would have been different, were I not to be gay and had to find my true gay self, there would still have been thorns along the way to the bed of roses. I am just glad my thorns were indeed rainbowed.

MIKE
51
HE/HIM/HIS

Love is love is love is love is love...

PASHA
51
SHE/HER OR THEY/THEM

Sorry I'm submitting this so late.

A final thought...

The Stonewall Uprising? The Marriage Equality Act? Something else?   200

DAVID
50
HE/HIM

I love you, Heather. Good luck with your book! ♥

MICHAEL
50
HE/HIM/HIS

Get involved in your community, in a cause. Be part of something that is bigger than you. It is a worthwhile investment and just might help you find yourself and your way.

KIMMY
47
HIM/HER

As someone who had hated themself for a long time and who finally surrendered to my true self, I've been left with a bunch of obstacles to overcome. Sure, I'm happier now because I'm not wasting my energy pretending to be straight. I am accepted/tolerated by my coworkers and the few friends I have. However, I am so late to the game and past my prime that I don't expect to find anyone who isn't just looking for a hookup. I live alone and I'll probably die alone. I was just starting to meet people and getting comfortable going to queer spaces. 2020 was going to be my year. I was going to focus on getting a date or at least a queer friend to hang with. COVID 19 destroyed all that. I will be 48 in a couple months. I will pretend to be happy.

JONATHAN
44
HE/HIM

There's a saying at the end of the movie, *The Broken Hearts Club,* said in voiceover:

"A lot of people ask me when I first knew I was gay. Fact is, I don't know. But what I do remember, what I can recall, is when I first realized it was okay. It was when I met these guys. My friends." This quote is still as important to me as it was when I first heard it twenty years ago. Every LGBTQ+ person will have a different coming out story and all are just as important and valid. Some come out as young people, some as adults. Some came out to supportive family, some were not accepted. But I feel what can really make the difference to someone's journey is friends. Looking back, my friends were integral to my journey and self-worth. I'm one of the lucky ones. Some aren't so lucky. Now, twenty years later and me being in my forties, I am honored to have a great network of family and friends, both born with and chosen. I love you all. In closing, let's honor the activists and icons that are on the front lines locally, fighting for our rights with little to no fanfare, and let's support our trans brothers and sisters more.

JV
43
HE/HIM/HIS

I'm so thankful for my family, even though my lifestyle wasn't accepted back then. The fact that I've come this far with the support I have speaks volumes. Just know that you are not alone. We are here for each other. All you need to do is reach out, and please know, it gets better! Don't let anyone ever tell you different. Hugs!

A final thought...

The Stonewall Uprising? The Marriage Equality Act? Something else?   200

KAYTI
LOOK 32, FEEL 78, LEGALLY 42
RECENTLY FEMALE (SHE/HER/HERS) TO EVERYONE BUT BLOOD FAMILY

Don't major in Taco Bell. It's a reference to being prepared in life and not just doing something for the social part. You're not always going to be accepted.

RYAN
39
HE/HIM

Thank you so much for including me on this. For those who are struggling with their own truths, I promise that life gets better, and that the freedom you will feel when you are released from that burden is truly magical!

STEPHEN
38
HE/HIM

ANDREW
30
PANSEXUAL TRANSGUY—HE/HIM

I am proud, grateful and at peace to be where I am, to be who I am, and for my journey! I still however struggle with it from time to time, depending on what's going on either in my personal life or in the world at any given time, but I wouldn't trade it for anything! Mental health, not just for me personally, but for the community as a whole, is an underlying problem I would say! I feel like stigmatization of mental illness is amplified with the LGBTQ community, due in part to the overall struggles we have with healthcare in general.

JACKSON
30
HE/HIM/HIS

MISS JESSICA
27
NON-BINARY, ALL PRONOUNS

Love people. Live authentically. Live unapologetically. Be loud. Be Proud.

PARRISH
23
HE/HIM

MADI
21
SHE/HER

Love is love, and we need to focus a lot more support to our Black and Brown brothers and sisters, our trans brothers and sisters, and our non-binary family members. Reach out, donate to good causes, and be a good person.

FREYA
20
SHE/HER/HERS

***

You are not alone—cheers to all of this!